50

# ★ The ★
# UNITED STATES
## AN ECONOMIC PERSPECTIVE

Victor A. Zelinski

Calgary Catholic School Board

Nigel M. Waters

University of Calgary

WILEY

**John Wiley & Sons**

Toronto   New York   Chichester   Brisbane   Singapore

**Canadian Cataloguing in Publication Data**
Zelinski, Victor A.
    The United States : an economic perspective

ISBN 0-471-79584-4

1. United States — Economic conditions.  I. Waters,
Nigel M. (Nigel Michael), 1950-  .  II. Title.

HC103.Z45 1990     330.973     C89-094744-9

Editor: Graham Draper
Copy Editor: Lisa Stacey
Designer: Julian Cleva
Illustrator: James Loates
Typesetter: Q Composition Inc.
Printer: TH Best

Printed and bound in Canada
10 9 8 7 6 5 4 3 2

Front cover: Top left, Ford Motor Company of Canada; top right, M. Stuckey/Miller Comstock Inc.; bottom, New York Convention & Visitors Bureau.

Back cover: Top left, Leonard M. Fanning, *Fathers of Industry*; top middle, The Bettmann Archive; top right, The Bettmann Archive; middle left, Library of Congress; middle right, Associated Press; bottom left, Ford Motor Company of Canada; bottom right, Birgitte Neilsen.

The cover photos are like an "instant replay" of the social and economic changes that have taken place in the United States. They depict the evolution of American industry from the first textile mills, through the development of the oil, rail, and automobile industries, to today's development of computer technologies and information management systems.

Looked at individually, the cover photos illustrate the enormous changes that have taken place in the labour force and in the relationship between the workers, unions, and management.

Think about each of these photos. Why do you think the authors chose them for the cover? Write down some of your thoughts. When you have completed this course, read your ideas again and compare them to what you now know about the United States and its economy.

# Contents

**SECTION 1   The Industrial Revolution and the United States   1**

**CHAPTER 1: The Industrial Revolution Begins in Britain   2**
Focus Questions   3
Concepts   3
Changes in Agriculture   3
Changes in Industry   6
Other Innovations of the Industrial Revolution   11
Summary   13
Checking Back   14
Understanding Concepts   14
Enrichment   14

**CHAPTER 2: The Industrial Revolution Spreads to North America   15**
Focus Questions   15
Concepts   16
The Movement of Industrial Knowledge to the United States   16
The Development of American Industries   18
Summary   23
Checking Back   23
Understanding Concepts   23
Enrichment   23

**CHAPTER 3: The Industrial Development of the United States   24**
Focus Questions   24
Concepts   24
Major Industries Trigger Change   25
The American Railroad Industry   25
The Oil Industry   29
Henry Ford and the American Automobile Industry   34
Summary   36
Checking Back   36
Understanding Concepts   37
Enrichment   37

**SECTION II   Physical and Economic Geography of the United States   38**

**CHAPTER 4: Physical Geography and Resources   40**
Focus Questions   40
Concepts   41
The Major Landscapes of the United States   41
Temperature, Precipitation, and Vegetation   47
Summary   50
Checking Back   50
Understanding Concepts   51
Enrichment   51

**CHAPTER 5: Geography, People, and Industry   52**
Focus Questions   52
Concepts   52
Settlement and Growth of the United States   53
Factors Affecting Industrial Locations   60
Summary   64
Checking Back   64
Understanding Concepts   64
Enrichment   65

**CHAPTER 6:   Government, Business, and Labour   66**
Focus Questions   66
Concepts   66
Government, Business, and Labour Institutions   67
The Role of Government in the American Economy   67
Business Corporations   71
Labour and Labour Organizations   76
Summary   79
Checking Back   79
Understanding Concepts   79
Enrichment   79

**SECTION III   The Market Economy of the United States   80**

**CHAPTER 7: The American Market Economy   82**
Focus Questions   83
Concepts   83
Economics: The Science of Scarcity   83
How the Market Economy Works   85
Summary   88
Checking Back   89
Understanding Concepts   89
Enrichment   89

**CHAPTER 8: The Entrepreneur   90**
Focus Questions   91
Concepts   91
The Characteristics of Entrepreneurs   91
Entrepreneurs and Managers   100
Summary   100
Checking Back   101
Understanding Concepts   101
Enrichment   101

**CHAPTER 9: The American Consumer   102**
Focus Questions   102
Concepts   102
Consumer Sovereignty   103
Consumer Issues in the American Market Economy   106
Summary   108
Checking Back   108
Understandiing Concepts   108
Enrichment   109

**SECTION IV   Life Today in the United States   110**

**CHAPTER 10: Environmental Issues   112**
Focus Questions   114
Concepts   114
Pollution   114
Protecting the Environment   121
Summary   123
Checking Back   123
Understanding Concepts   123
Enrichment   123

**CHAPTER 11: Economic Values and the Quality of Life   124**
Focus Questions   125
Concepts   125
Quality of Life in the United States   125
Sports in American Society   129
American Values and the Federal Budget Process   131
Summary   135
Checking Back   135
Understanding Concepts   135
Enrichment   135

**CHAPTER 12: Looking into the Future   136**
Focus Questions   136
Concepts   136
The Need to Predict Change   137
Changing Economic Patterns in the United States   138
Summary   141
Checking Back   142
Understanding Concepts   142
Enrichment   142

Glossary   143
Index   148
Sources   152

# Photo Credits

**Chapter 1**
Figure IA: British Museum.   Figure IB: TVOntario.
Figure 1A: Metropolitan Toronto Reference Library,
Picture Collection.   Figure 1.4: The Bettmann Archive.
Figure 1.5: Metropolitan Toronto Reference Library,
Picture Collection.   Figure 1.7: Textile Machinery Museum, Bolton Museum and Art Gallery.   Figure 1.8:
Metropolitan Toronto Reference Library, Picture
Collection.

**Chapter 2**
Figure 2A: Metropolitan Toronto Reference Library,
Picture Collection.   Figure 2.1: Leonard M. Fanning,
*Fathers of Industry*, p. 94.   Figure 2.2: Library of
Congress.   Figure 2.3: Metropolitan Toronto Reference
Library, Picture Collection.   Figure 2.4: Leonard M.
Fanning, *Fathers of Industry*, p. 105.   Figure 2.5: Metropolitan Toronto Reference Library, Picture Collection.   Figure 2.6: John Vanderlyn/New York Historical
Society.   Figure 2.7: Leonard M. Fanning, *Fathers of
Industry*, p. 81.

**Chapter 3**
Figure 3A: Library of Congress 2280-LC-US2-62-18103.
Figure 3.3: Metropolitan Toronto Reference Library,
Picture Collection.   Figure 3.6: Metropolitan Toronto
Reference Library, Picture Collection.   Figure 3.7:
The Bettmann Archive.   Figure 3.8: The Bettmann
Archive.   Figure 3.9: Ford Motor Company of Canada.
Figure 3.10: Ford Motor Company of Canada.

**Chapter 4**
Figure IIA: Canapress.   Figure 4A: Tom Walker/
Canapress.   Figure 4.4: The Bettmann Archive.
Figure 4.5: Canapress.

**Chapter 5**
Figure 5A: Ontario Hydro.   Figure 5.3: John Gast/
Library of Congress 2280-LC-US2-62-737.   Figure 5.4:
The Bettmann Archive.   Figure 5.5: Manitoba Archives
N8200.   Figure 5.6: Library of Congress.   Figure 5.9:
Department of Economic and Community Development, Maine.

**Chapter 6**
Figure 6A: Canapress.   Figure 6.2: The Bettmann
Archive.   Figure 6.7: Canapress.   Figure 6.8: Canapress.   Figure 6.11: Canapress.   Figure 6.12: The
Granger Collection.

**Chapter 7**
Figure IIIA: Canapress.   Figure IIIB: Canapress.
Figure 7A: Globe Photos.   Figure 7.2: Globe Photos.
Figure 7.6: Globe Photos.   Figure 7.7: J. Hart/Creators
Syndicate.

**Chapter 8**
Figure 8A: Robin Edgar/Canapress.   Figure 8.1: Canapress. Figure 8.2: Canapress.   Figure 8.3: Canapress.   Figure 8C: Apple Canada.   Figure 8.4: The
Bettmann Archive.   Figure 8.5: Apple Canada.   Figure
8.6: Apple Canada.   Figure 8.7: Mary Kay Cosmetics.
Figure 8D: Mary Kay Cosmetics.   Figure 8.8: Mary Kay
Cosmetics.

**Chapter 9**
Figure 9A: Globe Photos.   Figure 9.1: Canapress.
Figure 9.2: Coca-Cola Ltd.   Figure 9.3: Canapress.
Figure 9.4: Birgitte Nielsen.

**Chapter 10**
Figure IVA: J. LeBlanc/Canapress.   Figure IVB: Canapress.   Figure 10A: Canapress.   Figure 10B: Canapress.   Figure 10.1: Metropolitan Toronto Reference
Library, Picture Collection. Figure 10.2: Zachary Singer/
Greenpeace U.S.A.   Figure 10.8: Alex Williams/Greenpeace U.S.A.

**Chapter 11**
Figure 11A: Canapress.   Figure 11B: Bill Ivy.   Figure
11.1: Rick Reinhard.   Figure 11.3: Department of
Labor, U.S.A.   Figure 11.4: Canapress.   Figure 11.6:
Jay J. Coakley, *Sports in Society: Issues and
Controversies*, p. 78.   Figure 11.10: Birgitte Nielsen.

**Chapter 12**
Figure 12A: Terry W. Self/Canapress.

# Note to Students

Throughout the twentieth century, the United States has maintained its position as one of the strongest economies in the world. This strength was not accidental: the economic development of the United States came about as a result of a number of key factors. The nature of its economic system, a market economy, is one such factor. The purpose of this book is to give you an opportunity to investigate the conditions that led to the development of the American economy, to explore issues that arose out of its economic growth, and to determine how the quality of life in the United States is shaped by that growth. By studying the American situation, you will be better able to make more informed choices about Canadian and world issues that come from economic growth and change.

As you read through *The United States: An Economic Perspective*, think about these important questions:

- What were the important influences on the industrial development of the United States?
- How did changes in technology influence economic activities?
- What roles did entrepreneurs, labour organizations, and governments play in the economic development of the United States?
- What are the advantages and disadvantages for individuals in a market economy?

This book is organized into four sections. Section I (Chapters 1, 2, and 3) deals with historical factors that caused the Industrial Revolution and allowed it to spread to the United States. You will discover the conditions that were responsible for the rapid industrial growth of the American econ-omy. Section II (Chapters 4, 5, and 6) focusses on the physical, human, and economic geography of the country, particularly as it relates to the growth of industry.

In Section III (Chapters 7, 8, and 9), the nature and impact of the American market economy are explored. Chapters 7 and 8 deal with the characteristics of a market economy, the role of entrepreneurs, and the rights and responsibilities of consumers. The final section (Chapters 10, 11, and 12) analyses the economic values and issues related to the quality of life in the United States.

A number of features in this book help you investigate the topics. At the beginning of each chapter there are several broad questions that serve as a focus for your reading and inquiry. There is also a list of key concepts in each chapter to signal important ideas. Words that are printed in **bold type** are defined in the Glossary on pages 143-147. From time to time, you will encounter case studies and special issue investigations that encourage you to look more deeply at selected topics. As well, prominent people are profiled throughout the book to give you some insights into the personalities that helped to shape the American economy.

In each chapter there are several Progress Checks. Use these questions to make sure that you have understood the ideas covered to that point in the chapter. At the end of each chapter there are Checking Back and Understanding Concepts activities. These questions ask you to pull together all the ideas in the chapter, and then challenge you to think about how those ideas connect to other knowledge that you have.

Good luck with your investigations.

# Note to Teachers

This book's organization is designed to encourage students to use and to develop further their inquiry skills. Appropriate inquiry questions are posed at the beginning of each section and in the introduction to each chapter. As students work through each chapter's content and activities, they will encounter opportunities to develop such skills as critical reasoning, rational and informed decision making, distinguishing facts from opinions, and determining consequences of actions. Throughout, information and ideas are provided on the broad concepts of industrialization, market economy, and quality of life.

Experienced teachers will immediately see a great number of opportunities for creative teaching strategies using *The United States: An Economic Perspective* as a stimulus for inquiry and as a source of information. Teachers new to the curriculum emphases can consult the *Teacher's Manual*. It includes a variety of strategies and ideas to help implement the curriculum in classrooms.

Every effort has been made to avoid imbalances in references to race, ethnicity, sex, age, and belief systems.

# Acknowledgements

Many people contributed to the development of this book. In particular, we would like to thank Tony Burley, Valerie Doenz, Dirk Huysman, Phil Jensen, and Maria Steinborn for their constructive criticism and helpful suggestions. We also would like to thank the students who pilot tested the project in Central Junior High School in Red Deer, and Wilma Hansen Junior High School and Assumption Junior High School in Calgary.

Jason Zelinski researched many difficult aspects of the topics in preparing the manuscript, and Blake Springer spent hours at the keyboard producing the pilot version of the book. Graham Draper edited the manuscript while Elaine Freedman located the photographs we needed to make this book complete. Bob Kirk, Rena Leibovitch, and Elizabeth McCurdy of John Wiley & Sons were involved at all stages in the development of this project.

Finally, our thanks to Dr. Steven Lamy, University of Southern California, and Dr. Bob Stahl, Arizona State University, for their reviews of this project.

*Nigel Waters, Ph.D.*
*Victor A. Zelinski, B.A., M.Ed.*

# The Industrial Revolution and the United States

The Industrial Revolution began in Britain. By the 1780s, some key ideas and inventions from Britain had been carried to North America by skilled workers who emigrated to the New World. The industrialization of this frontier land led to the development of a new economic power, the United States of America.

The first chapter in this section explores the beginning of the Industrial Revolution in 18th century Britain. Chapter 2 continues the story by looking at the spread of the Industrial Revolution from Britain to North America. In the third chapter, you will study the impact of the Industrial Revolution on the United States.

**SECTION I**

**Chapter 1:** The Industrial Revolution Begins in Britain
**Chapter 2:** The Industrial Revolution Spreads to
            North America
**Chapter 3:** The Industrial Development of the United States

As you study this section of the book, keep these questions in mind:
• What changes did the Industrial Revolution bring to Britain and the United States?
• How did these changes affect people's lives?

# CHAPTER 1

# The Industrial Revolution Begins in Britain

In the history of the human race, two major changes occurred which forever altered the everyday lives of people. These changes were so significant that they are called revolutions. The first was the **Agricultural Revolution** which began about 10 000 years ago in the Middle East. Societies which for centuries had depended on hunting and gathering to obtain food, clothing and shelter began to provide for their basic physical needs by **domesticating** plants and animals.

Agriculture had a number of advantages over hunting and gathering. First, it gave a more secure source of food. Hunting required skill, endurance, and luck; failure could result in starvation. Raising cattle, sheep, or other animals gave people a more reliable supply of food and clothing. Similarly, people who cultivated plants instead of gathering fruits and vegetables had a better chance of ensuring a good supply of food.

Second, agricultural surplus could be stored for times of scarcity. A secure and plentiful supply of food encouraged population growth.

Third, the production of food took much less time and energy. As a result, people had time to develop their special skills and talents to become artisans, merchants, and traders. When people in a society specialize according to their interests or skills, it is called a **division of labour**.

Most nations have long since passed through the Agricultural Revolution, although it is still going on in some parts of the world. There are still some **nomadic** people in remote areas of the world who live off the land. They are hunters and gatherers who use the natural game and vegetation to meet their basic needs for food, clothing, and shelter.

The second revolution or major change that affected the way in which people lived started in Britain in the late 1700s and became known as the **Industrial Revolution**. This term is used to describe the changes that occur when a society industrializes. The first nation to go through these changes was Britain. The changes took place over a period of several decades and gradually spread to other countries.

## FOCUS QUESTIONS

1. **Why did the Industrial Revolution start in Britain?**
2. **Who were the key inventors and entrepreneurs of the Industrial Revolution?**
3. **How did the Industrial Revolution change the way people worked and lived in Britain?**

## CONCEPTS

| | |
|---|---|
| Agricultural Revolution | entrepreneurs |
| division of labour | capital |
| Industrial Revolution | factory system |
| Enclosure Acts | |
| cottage industry | |
| patent | |

# Changes in Agriculture

Britain, in 1700, was largely a rural, agricultural society. Most people lived on farms. They worked long hours growing their own food, making their own clothing, and collecting firewood to warm their houses in the damp, cold climate. Life was simple and hard. Most people were very poor and, if the harvest failed, they risked starvation. There were no organized social welfare programs, medical practices were primitive, sickness and disease were common, infant mortality was high, and the average life expectancy was low. All of this was to change.

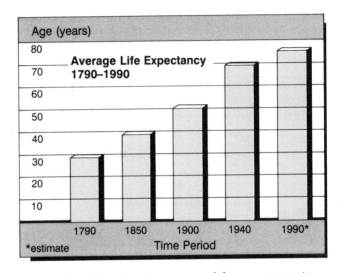

**Figure 1.1** *How has the average life expectancy in Britain changed since 1790? State the 1990 life expectancy as a percentage of the 1790 figure.*

## Enlarging the Farms

Between 1760 and 1830, much of the farmland in Britain was consolidated into large farms through a series of measures called the **Enclosure Acts** which were passed by the British Parliament. The purpose of the Acts (the first of which were passed in the 1500s) was to make farming more efficient. Over the centuries, the farmland in Britain had been divided and subdivided into a

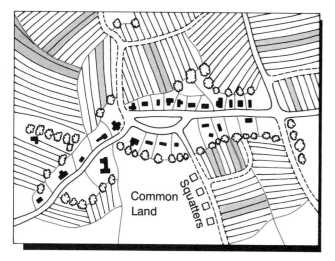

**Figure 1.2** *Farming in Britain before the Enclosure Acts*

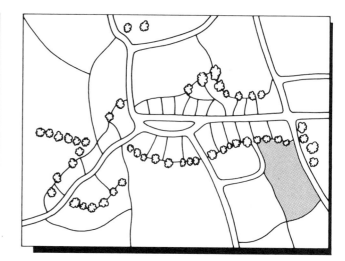

**Figure 1.3** *Enclosure consolidated the farmland into large, more efficient units. Who benefited from this action?*

large number of small strips as shown in Figure 1.2. This happened for several reasons. Large landowners with several children might divide the land among them, and farmers bought and sold small strips from one another. In time, wealthier farmers owned a number of small strips of land scattered around the village. Many wealthier farmers felt they needed to consolidate the scattered pieces of land so that efficient, large-scale production techniques could be used.

Large blocks of common land were available for community use. This land was particularly important to farmers with small farms because they had the right to graze their animals on it. Also, they had **gleaning rights**. This meant they could gather wood for fuel in the woodlands and pick up any leftover grain after the harvest. The farmers with larger farms thought that the common lands could be put to better use. They knew that if the common lands were "enclosed" by Parliament, the small peasant farmers would not be able to continue to farm on their small strips of land and would have to sell. The net effect would be a redistribution of the small strip farms into larger, more efficient units.

Gradually, the wealthiest landowners got their way, and the Enclosure Acts were passed. Parliament at that time was controlled entirely by men who owned property, and they established the rule that an Enclosure Act would be approved if the owners of at least three-fourths of the land in the area agreed. Of course, this meant that one or two of the wealthiest landowners could outvote a large number of small farmers.

After the land was enclosed, all farmers were allocated new land according to how much they had owned previously, but now all their land was in a single parcel. Most of the common lands and the woodlands were enclosed. Those people who had little or no land of their own and relied on the use of the common land lost that privilege. As compensation, everyone was given an additional small parcel of land; however, this land was often inadequate for farmers' needs, so many of these people simply sold their land to large landowners. The small farmers could not afford to fence it anyway, something required by the Enclosure Acts. A major result of enclosure was that many of the poor people moved from rural areas to cities to look for work.

The effect of the enclosures was dramatic. A class of wealthy landowners developed who rented their land to tenant farmers. The average size of these tenant farms ranged from 40 to 200 ha, much larger than holdings before enclosure. These farms were large by European standards. For example, the average size of farms in France at this time was 5 ha, while German farms were even smaller. This made the English farmer more efficient and competitive than any other farmer in the world.

## PROGRESS CHECK

1. **Why were the Enclosure Acts passed?**
2. **What effects did these enclosures have on small and large farms?**
3. **How did the voting procedures to decide on enclosures favour the large landowners? Do you think this system was fair?**
4. **What was the effect of the Enclosure Acts on farm efficiency in Britain?**

# Changes in Agricultural Methods

The Enclosure Acts created large, efficient farms run by wealthy farmers who were willing and able to try new ideas. Two such farmers, Viscount **Charles Townshend** and **Jethro Tull**, increased the efficiency of farming methods with two innovations during this period.

Townshend introduced a new system of crop rotation. Traditionally, crops were grown in a three-field system over a three-year period. This system is shown in Table 1.1.

**Table 1.1** *The Three-Field Crop Rotation System*

|         | YEAR 1             | YEAR 2  | YEAR 3 |
|---------|--------------------|---------|--------|
| Field 1 | Wheat              | Barley  | Fallow |
| Field 2 | Barley             | Fallow  | Wheat  |
| Field 3 | Fallow<br>(no crop) | Wheat   | Barley |

With the three-field system, there were only two fields with crops. Each field's soil recovered its fertility during its fallow year when no crop was sown. Townshend introduced a four-year rotation cycle using four crops, each sown in separate fields. The crops were rotated to a different field each year, so a field was never fallow. Instead, adding manure and sowing a crop of clover helped to restore the fields' fertility. Townshend's system is outlined in Table 1.2.

**Table 1.2** *Townshend's Four-Year Rotation Cycle*

| YEAR   | CROP PLANTED                                                                                       |
|--------|---------------------------------------------------------------------------------------------------|
| Year 1 | Wheat—basic crop but reduces soil fertility                                                        |
| Year 2 | Turnip—provides food for sheep (The sheep then provide manure for the soil to restore fertility)   |
| Year 3 | Barley—requires fertile soil and reduces the fertility                                             |
| Year 4 | Clover—provides nitrogen for soil fertility and food for cattle (The cattle manure also helps to restore fertility) |

The new system was much more productive, yet no more harmful to the land. Growing turnips and clover as food for cattle and sheep also gave farmers additional sources of income.

Jethro Tull introduced machinery to farming in Britain. The old **broadcasting** method of planting by scattering seeds by hand was inefficient. Seeds were scattered thickly in some places, while other places received no seeds at all. To correct this problem, Tull developed a seed planting machine that deposited seeds at the proper depth and in straight rows. Crops planted in rows could be weeded easily and harvested by other machines. Tull's seed drill also ensured that more seeds germinated because they were automatically covered with soil. As well, Tull developed a new plough and prepared the way for a whole new industry devoted to the development of agricultural machinery.

The improvements that Townshend, Tull, and others made in agricultural methods were very important. These innovations made farms more productive and efficient. Fewer people were needed to work on the farms to provide food for the country. While machines displaced workers on the farms, extra jobs were created in the towns and cities making the machines; thus, changes in agriculture helped spur the Industrial Revolution.

## PROGRESS CHECK

1. **Why was Townshend's four-crop rotation more efficient than the three-crop rotation?**
2. **Briefly describe the innovations developed by Jethro Tull.**

# Changes in Industry

How did changes in agriculture affect the development of the Industrial Revolution? One important factor was the creation of a large, urban labour force. Most of the poor, displaced farmers moved to the growing cities where they tried to find work. New coal mines and factories were starting to open up, and they all required workers. Workers were also hired to build the roads, canals, and railroads that moved the goods and people. In short, the Enclosure Acts and agricultural innovations created a large pool of labour that would provide the "muscle" for the Industrial Revolution.

The Industrial Revolution was fuelled primarily by changes in a few key industries. Two such industries were textiles and transportation. In each of these industries, a series of new inventions made a tremendous impact on Britain and, eventually, the world. These inventions stimulated and supported each other, causing enormous growth in British industry from the late 1700s to the mid-1800s.

# Inventions in the Textile Industry

Historians have suggested that it was the textile industry that made Britain the most advanced and prosperous industrial nation of the early 1800s. In the early 1700s, spinning and weaving were **cottage industries**, so named because, at this time, almost all manufacturing was done by hand at home. If you needed clothing, you made it. If you needed an article of furniture, you made it. Very few items were bought from a store, so it was natural to spin yarn and make clothing in one's home.

Two people who made important changes to the textile industry were **John Kay** and **James Hargreaves**. Their inventions moved the industry from the cottage to the factory. John Kay invented the "flying shuttle" in 1733, replacing the hand-held shuttle used in weaving. This machine doubled the amount of cloth a weaver could make; however, the weavers could only work as fast as the spinners who made the yarn. A machine that would spin yarn faster was needed. Finally, in 1765, James Hargreaves built the first "spinning jenny." One story suggests that he invented the spinning jenny when his daughter Jenny accidentally knocked over his spinning wheel. He found that the spindle, which was normally horizontal, would continue to work in a vertical position. Hargreaves built a frame around his spinning wheel so that more than one spindle could be used at a time. Early models of his invention had up to eight spindles. This allowed one spinner to produce eight times as much thread. The new spinning machines became very popular and eventually had as many as 120 spindles. This greatly increased the amount of thread that could be produced, so now the weavers had a good supply of thread for their work. The invention of the spinning jenny marks the beginning of the Industrial Revolution.

In 1770, Hargreaves tried to **patent** his invention. A patent grants an inventor ownership

**Figure 1.4** *An improved model of Hargreaves' spinning jenny*

of an invention. The inventor can then sell to others the right to copy and use the invention. In Hargreaves' case, this would have meant that only he, or those people who paid him a fee, would have the right to build spinning jennies. The patent would have made him a rich man, but his application was denied on a technicality. Apparently, he sold some of his jennies before he applied for the patent. Because of this, Hargreaves made very little profit from his invention. He died in 1778 a relatively poor man.

## PROGRESS CHECK

1. **What is a cottage industry?**
2. **How did the invention of the flying shuttle lead to the invention of the spinning jenny?**
3. **What does it mean to patent an invention?**

## Sir Richard Arkwright and the Factory System

The success of the textile industry increased with the inventions of **Richard Arkwright**. He was born in 1732 in the small town of Preston in northeast England. He began the manufacture of a new spinning machine similar to the jenny, but which used sets of rollers to draw cotton from the carding machine. This process produced a much stronger thread. Arkwright's machine was called a **water frame** because it was powered by water. For the first time, a textile machine was being powered by an energy source other than a person or an animal. The use of new sources of energy to run machines was an important feature of the Industrial Revolution. It increased the quantity of goods produced without increasing the number of workers needed.

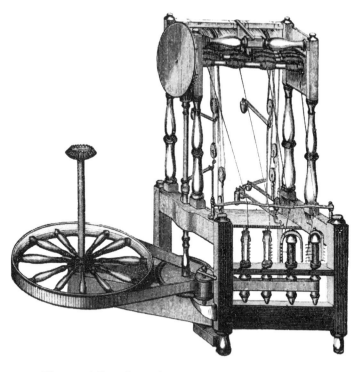

**Figure 1.5** *Arkwright's water frame. What was important about the use of water with this new invention?*

Arkwright's mill at Cromford, built in 1771, marked the beginning of the **factory system** of employment. In this system, employees came to the workplace, in contrast to the cottage industry where employees worked in their homes. The factory system changed the way millions of people lived and worked.

For the owner, the factory system was an enormous success. Workers could be disciplined to start at a certain time and to do specific tasks. The division of work into specific tasks, known as division of labour, increased production; however, from the point of view of the workers, the factory system was less successful. Many factories were run with harsh rules that exploited the workers. They earned low wages and were forced to live in the slums of dirty cities. For many, the **quality of life** was much worse than it had been before factories were developed. Quality of life refers to the things that make life worthwhile, such as a person's happiness, satisfaction, and peace of mind. People living in slum housing and working in dreary factories had a poor quality of life. Eventually, the British Parliament passed laws to protect workers from the worst abuses in factories, and created social welfare programs for the poor.

Unlike Hargreaves who died poor, Arkwright prospered from his invention. He was a shrewd business person and an example of a successful **entrepreneur**. Entrepreneurs are people who are willing to take risks in order to make profits. Arkwright willingly risked his own money to develop his original water frame. He persuaded a banker to provide him with money or **capital** to finance the manufacture of his machines. In addition, he persuaded the government to remove the **duty**, or tax, on cloth. Since this made cloth cheaper, he sold more of it.

Arkwright's business prospered and he built a number of mills which eventually employed as many as 5000 workers. The mills were located in specific places for economic reasons, near water for a cheap supply of power or near a railway line so the products could be moved easily.

Arkwright was regarded as an enlightened factory owner who took care of his employees, but this did not prevent some people from attacking his factories. When he built a new steam-powered factory at Chorley, a mob burned it to the ground. These people, called Luddites, objected to the new factory system and wanted to turn the clock back. They argued that the factory system increased unemployment, created low wages, and produced poorer quality goods. In spite of their protests, the factory system was there to stay.

Arkwright worked long days of up to 16 hours and prospered without a formal education. He died in 1792, a respected man who had been knighted by King George III.

# RULES
## TO BE OBSERVED
### By the Hands Employed in
# THIS MILL.

RULE

1. All the Overlookers shall be on the premises first and last.
2. Any Person coming too late shall be fined as follows:—for 5 minutes 2d, 10 minutes 4d, and 15 minutes 6d. &c.
3. For any Bobbins found on the floor 1d for each Bobbin.
5. For Waste on the floor 2d.
6. For any Oil wasted or spilled on the floor 2d each offence, besides paying for the value of the Oil.
7. For any broken Bobbins, they shall be paid for according to their value, and if there is any difficulty in ascertaining the guilty party, the same shall be paid for by the whole using such Bobbins.
8. Any person neglecting to Oil at the proper times shall be fined 2d.
9. Any person leaving their Work and found Talking with any of the other workpeople shall be fined 2d for each offence.
10. For every Oath or insolent language, 3d for the first offence and if repeated they shall be dismissed.
11. The Machinery shall be swept and cleaned down every meal time.
12. All persons in our employ shall serve Four Weeks' Notice before leaving their employ; but L. WHITAKER & SONS shall and will turn any person off without notice being given.
16. The Masters would recommend that all their workpeople Wash themselves every morning, but they shall Wash themselves at least twice every week, Monday morning and Thursday morning; and any found not washed will be fined 3d for each offence.
18. Any persons found smoking on the premises will be instantly dismissed.
19. Any person found away from their usual place of work, except for necessary purposes, or Talking with any one out of their own Alley will be fined 2d for each offence.
21. Any person wilfully damaging this Notice will be dismissed.

The Overlookers are strictly enjoined to attend to these Rules, and they will be responsible to the Masters for the Workpeople observing them.

WATER-FOOT MILL, NEAR HASLINGDEN.
September, 1851.

J. Read, Printer, and Bookbinder, Haslingden

**Figure 1.6** *Mill rules in 1851*

**PROGRESS CHECK**

1. **What was the significance of the water frame?**
2. **What is an entrepreneur?**
3. **Briefly explain what is meant by the factory system.**
4. **What were some of the positive and negative effects of the factory system?**
5. **What is meant by quality of life? Demonstrate your understanding of the phrase by using it in a sentence.**

## Samuel Crompton

There were many other inventors who helped to mechanize the textile industry. In 1779, **Samuel Crompton** produced a machine which combined the best aspects of Hargreaves' jenny and Arkwright's water frame. This machine was called a "mule" because a mule is a cross between a horse and a donkey, combining the best characteristics of each. Like the jenny, the mule stretched the thread, making it very fine and, like the frame, it produced a very strong thread that would resist breaking.

Samuel Crompton was not a rich man and could not afford to obtain a patent on the mule or to fight the legal challenges which seemed to accompany patent applications. As a result, he agreed to show the public his new machine in return for a "generous sum of money." This turned out to be £60, a sum equal to about two years of wages for a working family. But his invention changed the industry, and by 1812, 80 percent of all cotton spun in Britain was being spun on a mule; thus, Britain became the centre of the world's cotton industry.

In 1812, the British government gave Crompton a prize of £5000 for his efforts. This substantial sum of money was enough for him to pay his debts, and live comfortably until his death in 1827.

Crompton was a good inventor but a poor business person. He lacked the skills of an entrepreneur and so did not benefit greatly from his invention and business enterprises. In order for people to take full advantage of a new invention, they have to be able to sell it to others. They need the support of banks and people who have money, and they need patent protection so that others will not copy their idea. They may also need the support of the government to create a suitable environment for the growth of the business. Some inventors have the skills to be successful entrepreneurs while others do not.

**PROGRESS CHECK**

1. **How did Samuel Crompton's mule change the textile industry?**
2. **In order to make money from an invention, what does an inventor need to do?**

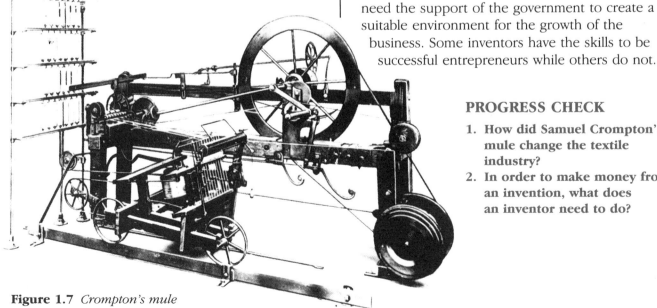

**Figure 1.7** *Crompton's mule*

## Inventions in the Provision of Power

The earliest textile factories used running water to power their machines. This meant that the factories had to be built beside streams. In addition to restricting the sites where textile factories could be built, water power had another drawback. In times of drought, streams ran low or dried up, decreasing or stopping the power to the factories. The solution to this problem was a new invention—**steam power**.

Arkwright was one of the first to use steam power to operate textile machinery, but his steam engine had limited uses and was not very practical. It was **James Watt** who developed the potential of the steam engine. He was a Scottish engineer who laboured for four years to design the new machine. Watt received a patent for his invention in 1769. Later, he teamed up with **Matthew Boulton**, who owned the Soho Engineering works in Birmingham, and formed the Boulton and Watt Company.

Watt made and patented numerous improvements to the steam engine. He invented a rotary steam engine that delivered smooth power and, therefore, proved useful for textile machinery.

Watt also invented a clever method of estimating the power of his steam engines. He calculated that a horse could lift 14.85 t a distance of about one-third of a metre in one minute. By comparison, his steam engine had a capacity of 40 horses or 40 horsepower. Watt used this information to market the engines. It was such a popular method of determining the power of an engine that it is still used today to measure the performance of engines. Watt died a rich and respected man in 1819 at the age of 83.

# Other Innovations of the Industrial Revolution

It would be difficult to discuss all the innovations of the Industrial Revolution in Britain in a book of this size. It is important, however, to look at two other industries: transportation and iron making. Both of these industries had a major impact on other industries that were beginning to develop.

## Innovations in the Transportation Industry

The transportation industry provided an important link between producers and suppliers. Products grown or manufactured in one area of the country had to be moved to markets in other areas. The best markets were the rapidly growing cities. Transportation allowed supply to meet demand.

Improvements in industries were closely linked to improvements in transportation. Efficient transportation encouraged industry because it allowed raw materials to be gathered from various places. For example, the iron and steel industries required coal, limestone, and iron ore as raw materials. These minerals were often found in different places and had to be transported to a convenient manufacturing point.

During the 1700s, transportation in Britain improved for a number of reasons. First, Parliament gave people permission to form Turnpike Trusts if they would undertake to improve local roads. Gates or turnpikes were installed on the roads and travellers were charged a fee as they passed through each gate.

Second, new methods of constructing roads were developed. Turnpike Trusts hired engineers such as **John McAdam** to develop new ways of building roads. McAdam built roads that were well drained and had hard surfaces. This meant that they lasted longer and were less likely to become rutted by the wheels of heavy coaches.

A third reason is that road transportation became better organized. Forests were cleared away from the edges of roads. This reduced the likelihood of people being attacked by highwaymen who would lurk in the trees, hidden from view. Hostelries and hotels were built at strategic staging points. These allowed travellers rest and refreshment while fresh horses were harnessed to the coach.

Fourth, Britain built many canals. Waterways were connected by canals, creating an efficient system of cheap transportation. The most important of the early canals were those built by the **Duke of Bridgewater** from his estate at Worsley to Manchester, and from Manchester to Runcorn on the English coast near Liverpool. These canals were used to transport coal. Canals were built throughout Britain and proved to be a very efficient method of transport as shown in Table 1.3.

**Table 1.3** *The Load One Horse Could Pull Using Different Forms of Transportation*

| METHOD OF TRANSPORTATION | LOAD PULLED |
|---|---|
| Pack horse | 125 kg |
| Stage wagon—soft road | 600 kg |
| Stage wagon—MacAdamized hard road | 1800 kg |
| Barge on river | 2700 kg |
| Barge on canal | 4500 kg |

One of the most important developments in the transport industry was the coming of the railroads. This will be discussed in Chapter 3 when it is examined in relation to the growth of the American railroad system.

**Figure 1.8** *Transportation improvements stimulated economic activities throughout Britain*

## Inventions in the Iron Industry

Iron metal was originally **smelted** from the waste rock through the use of charcoal in a furnace. The charcoal furnaces were small and inefficient and, as the demand for charcoal grew, the wood used to make the charcoal was soon in short supply. A new technology was needed to make iron that did not require charcoal. As is so often the case, necessity is the mother of invention. In 1709, **Abraham Darby** met this challenge when he discovered how to use coke, a purified form of coal, to smelt the iron ore.

The use of coke to produce iron created a new product called **cast iron**. Products such as pots, pans, and cannons could be cast using moulds. The new process required that air be blown into the furnace. In 1775, **John Wilkinson**, another English iron master, successfully used a steam engine to do this. Finally, in 1783 and 1784, **Henry Cort** developed and patented his **puddling** and **rolling** processes to remove the impurities in cast iron and to produce a stronger, more malleable, **wrought iron**. Wrought iron was better suited for tools and other goods like nails.

As the iron industry shows, one innovation usually leads to others. There have been many developments in the processing of iron ore since the 1700s, all tending to improve quality and reduce production costs.

### PROGRESS CHECK

1. **Why were the iron and transport industries so important?**
2. **What is a canal? Why were canals developed?**
3. **List three developments that helped produce better iron.**
4. **Based on Table 1.3, which form of transportation is cheapest?**

## Financing the Industrial Revolution

Who pays to develop an invention? Before the Industrial Revolution, it was very difficult to raise money for new businesses since wealth was concentrated in the hands of a conservative aristocracy. During the Industrial Revolution, there was a demand for capital for new industries. Wealthy landowners and factory owners took advantage of this demand, and the number of lending banks increased greatly. Borrowing money from a bank became a common way of raising money to finance a new invention. It became increasingly more popular during the 1700s as the number of banks expanded.

A second method of raising money was to sell **shares** in a company. Abraham Darby set up his company casting iron pots by selling shares. While this method allows money to be obtained quickly and easily, the company becomes a **public company**. The inventor must share control of the company with the people who have invested in it.

A third way of raising money was to arrange loans from private sources, such as friends and relatives.

# Summary

There is no doubt that the changes which occurred in Britain in the 18th century had a major effect on the lives of people. Agriculture became more efficient, which led to increased crop surpluses. Wealthy landowners accumulated capital and used it to develop new ideas. Inventors such as Arkwright and Hargreaves mechanized the textile industry and helped to create a factory system which employed the people displaced by the Enclosure Acts. While many people suffered during these changes, Britain did become a powerful industrial nation. The changes in Britain soon spread to Europe and North America.

# Checking Back

1. Assume the role of a displaced farmer or a wealthy landowner. Write a letter to a friend or family member in a distant town explaining the effects of the Enclosure Acts.
2. Using the information in this chapter, create a web of inventions that shows how one invention tends to lead to others.
3. In a short essay, compare the factory system of production to cottage industries. Include the advantages and disadvantages of each system of production.

## TIME LINE

**1700**
**1709** —Darby uses coke to smelt iron
**1730s** —Viscount Townshend develops the four-year crop rotation cycle
**1733** —Tull publishes book on scientific farming
**1750**
**1765** —Hargreaves builds the first spinning jenny
**1769** —Arkwright obtains patent on his frame spinning machine
**1779** —Crompton builds the first mule
**1781** —Watt invents the rotary action steam engine
**1800**

# Understanding Concepts

4. Copy this table into your notebook and fill in the details to show the importance of four specific inventions to the Industrial Revolution.

| INVENTION | INVENTOR | DATE | IMPORTANCE |
|---|---|---|---|
| seed drill | | | |
| spinning jenny | | | |
| water frame | SAMPLE ONLY | | |
| steam engine | | | |

5. Find an example of a recent invention and predict what effect it might have in the near future.

# Enrichment

6. Using reference books, find an invention that was important to the Industrial Revolution that was not discussed in this chapter. Write a short paragraph identifying the importance of the invention and the inventor to the Industrial Revolution.
7. A number of writers wrote about Britain during the 17th and 18th centuries, such as Charles Dickens. Find examples of the works of such writers. How have they described the quality of life of the common people?
8. Writers such as **Alvin Toffler** argue that there is now a third revolution underway, the **Information Revolution**. It is based on computers and micro-electronics. He claims that this revolution will affect our lives in a dramatic way, perhaps causing a return to the cottage industry which existed before the Industrial Revolution. What are the cottage industries of today? What kinds of jobs are found in modern cottage industries? How will people be affected?
9. Research the meaning of the term ''Neo-Luddites''.

# CHAPTER 2

# *The Industrial Revolution Spreads to North America*

**T**he Industrial Revolution began in Britain and spread to other parts of the world, including Europe and North America. Many inventions and ideas that were developed in Britain were taken to North America by immigrants who settled in the new land. These ideas spurred the development of American industry. This chapter tells the story of the spread of the Industrial Revolution to the United States.

**FOCUS QUESTIONS**

1. **How did the new technologies of the Industrial Revolution in Britain spread to the United States?**
2. **Who were the leading inventors and entrepreneurs who prepared the way for the American Industrial Revolution?**

## CONCEPTS

industrialization    interchangeability of parts
mechanization       division of labour
mass production     transportation

# The Movement of Industrial Knowledge to the United States

Britain became the world's leading industrial power because of the Industrial Revolution. Its political and business leaders wanted to maintain this advantage. For a long time, Britain tried to prevent the spread of industrial technology to other countries. The British were particularly concerned that the new technologies not spread to the colonies in North America. These colonies were an excellent market for the cottons and other textiles produced in British factories. If the colonies started to manufacture their own cloth, this important market would be lost; therefore, the British government did all that it could to prevent skilled workers from taking plans for the new textile machinery to the American colonies.

How could they do this? An important way was to impose stiff penalties on people caught smuggling plans and blueprints of the new machines out of the country. Laws were passed to prohibit skilled workers from emigrating to the American colonies. In the 1780s, workers who did try to emigrate lost their British citizenship and property. The Americans, on the other hand, used recruiting agents to entice British workers to the colonies. The British countered by passing a law that made such recruiting an offence. A recruiting agent could be fined £500 and put in jail for 12 months for each worker who emigrated to the colonies; however, these laws were not effective in stopping the trickle of emigrants from Britain to the United States. Perhaps the greatest loss to Britain came when **Sam Slater** emigrated to America.

## Sam Slater

Sam Slater was born in 1768, the son of a wealthy Derbyshire farmer. At the age of 15, he became an apprentice in a textile mill. Slater worked hard and before he was halfway through his training, he was promoted to the position of overseer in the mill. During this period, he found out through recruiting agents and newspapers that the Americans were willing to pay very well for skilled textile workers, especially workers who could repair machinery. One Philadelphia newspaper reported that the legislature offered a reward of £100 for anyone who could produce replacement parts for Hargreaves' spinning jenny. Slater vowed that once he had completed his six-and-a-half-year apprenticeship, he would be off to America, the land of promise.

In 1789, at the age of 21, Slater sailed to the newly independent United States. He did not need to take technical drawings of textile machines with him because he had memorized all the details. He did, however, need his apprenticeship papers to prove to the Americans that he was a skilled textile worker, so he sewed these into the lining of his coat. In order to avoid detection by British officials, Slater disguised

**Figure 2.1** *Moses Brown's mill at Pawtucket, Rhode Island, was the first successful textile mill in North America, thanks to the technical skill of Sam Slater.*

himself as a farmer and boarded a vessel in London. After a trip of 66 days, he landed in New York in November, 1789.

Slater soon found work in the United States. When he heard that **Moses Brown**, a Quaker from Pawtucket, Rhode Island, was having trouble with his textile machines, he wrote to Brown offering to help with a money-back guarantee. He said, "If I do not make as good a yarn as they do in England, I will have nothing for my services." Brown admired his spirit and hired him; however, Slater immediately regretted his promise. In Britain, he could have easily completed the repair work because there were plenty of factories capable of producing the necessary parts, but this was not the case in the United States. To solve the problem, Brown introduced Slater to **Orziel Wilkinson** who, together with his four sons, owned an iron foundry. The foundry was

primitive compared to the British factories, but the Wilkinsons were extremely skilled workers and they were able to build all the parts. Slater drew the plans for the parts entirely from memory.

In December, 1790, only 13 months after he had landed in New York, Slater had Brown's 72-spindle mill operating properly. It was America's first successful textile mill. He rebuilt the mill three years later when it became inadequate to meet the demand for cloth.

Slater went on to build other mills in partnership with **David Wilkinson**, son of Orziel Wilkinson. By 1809, there were 17 mills around Providence, Rhode Island, with a capacity of 14 290 spindles. Slater and others later expanded the number of mills throughout the other New England states.

The picture of Slater's first mill shows that it

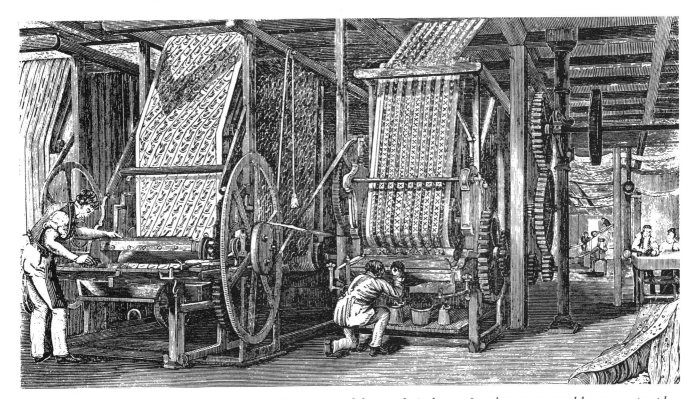

**Figure 2.2** *New machines greatly increased the output of the textile industry. In what ways would average people have benefited from these improvements?*

**17**

is situated on a stream. Water power was essential for the new textile machines. The New England states were particularly fortunate because they had a large number of streams which could supply the needed power. This important aspect quickly established New England as the major centre of the textile industry in North America. Other aspects of New England's geography and politics which helped this new industry to expand included:

- nearby markets in Boston and New York;
- excellent water transportation to these markets;
- nearby sources of raw materials for the factories; and
- a trade embargo on the importing of textiles brought into effect in 1807.

Sam Slater died on April 20, 1835. He has been labelled "The Founder of the American Textile Industry." His importance cannot be overestimated because the textile industry was America's first large-scale industry. It did much to establish the economic independence of the United States, and was one of the foundations upon which other industries were built. It remains one of the most important industries in the United States.

## PROGRESS CHECK

1. **How did Sam Slater bring technical knowledge about the textile machinery from Britain to the United States?**
2. **Give reasons to explain why the mill at Pawtucket is considered "the cradle of American industry."**
3. **List five factors that made New England the centre of the textile industry.**
4. **Was the British government right in passing laws to prevent the export of industrial technology? Were they right to try to prevent skilled textile workers, such as Slater, from emigrating? Prepare a list of arguments for and against the government's actions. Which side of the issue do you favour?**

# The Development of American Industries

The period immediately following the American War of Independence is known as the Post-Colonial Period. It represents the very beginning of the growth of American industry and economic power. During that time, a number of industries provided the basis for further industrial expansion. In each case, there were a variety of factors which contributed to the growth of these industries, and a number of key people who helped these industries to grow rapidly.

## The Small Arms Industry

The small arms industry developed rapidly in the American colonies during the War of Independence. When hostilities broke out between the colonists and the British in 1775, the British navy blockaded the North American colonies. The blockade was designed to prevent armaments from reaching the rebels, forcing the Americans to make their own weapons.

Making weapons and precision tools was a problem at this time because everything was made by hand. Each item was custom-made by craftspeople; parts were not interchangeable. Two developments had to occur before the small arms industry could really grow. The first was the development of the machine tool industry and the second was the invention of mass production techniques.

### THE MACHINE TOOL INDUSTRY

David Wilkinson, a partner of Sam Slater, is widely acknowledged as the founder of the machine tool industry. Born in 1771, he was recognized as a mechanical genius from childhood. At the age of nine, he worked full-time in his father's blacksmith shop. At 23, he and another mechanic installed a Boulton and Watt steam engine in a

**Figure 2.3** *Traditional methods of production were slow, as each part had to be custom-fitted. New machines and new techniques developed during the Industrial Revolution changed arms manufacturing forever.*

small boat and attached rough paddles to the drive mechanism. The steamboat was born. A shortage of funds prevented Wilkinson from working on the steamboat. Instead, he concentrated his efforts on the design of a **sliding rest lathe** for cutting screws. The lathe holds the cutting tool, not the worker, making the task of cutting and shaping screws more accurate and ensuring a more standard product.

In 1798, Wilkinson secured the patent for his new machine, but failed to protect it. While this oversight did little to help Wilkinson financially, it did much to help the rapid growth of the machine tool industry.

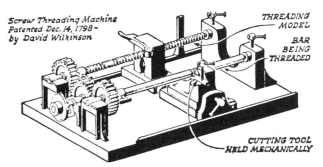

**Figure 2.4** *Wilkinson's patented screw-threading machine. How did it work?*

Wilkinson spent much of his working life in the machine tool shops which he, his brothers, and father ran to supply and repair the machines in Sam Slater's textile factories. These shops became training grounds for apprentices who learned the new skills of machining parts for industry, and then set up shops of their own. These men were widely referred to as "Wilkinson men"; thus, Wilkinson not only developed new ideas, machines, and technology, but he also taught others.

In his later life, Wilkinson suffered several financial setbacks, but his spirit remained undaunted. In his book, *Reminiscences*, he recalls how, at the age of 65, he was forced to seek work as a labourer on various construction projects. In 1848, 50 years after he had patented the sliding rest lathe, the United States Congress voted him an award of $10 000 for "benefits accruing to the public service." Wilkinson died on February 3, 1852, at the age of 81. He was never rich, even with his prize money, but he was widely respected.

## PROGRESS CHECK

1. **Why is Wilkinson regarded as the founder of the machine tool industry?**
2. **How did Wilkinson's apprenticeship program help to promote the use of machines and new technology in the United States?**
3. **Why did the American government award a prize to Wilkinson?**

## MASS PRODUCTION TECHNIQUES

The work of Wilkinson and others like him who helped to establish the machine tool industry cannot be overemphasized. It was these people who developed machines to cut, grind, and drill, and who expanded single tool machines into multiple tool machines. The new machines had greater power and speed, and operated with much higher tolerances than ever before. They could turn out parts with the same precision over and over again. With the new machines came new production techniques to take advantage of innovations. One of the most important people in the development of these **mass production techniques** was **Eli Whitney**.

Eli Whitney was born in 1765 in Westborough, Massachusetts. His father was a farmer who also owned a forge and prospered making nails during the War of Independence. After the war was over, Eli, who was only 15, developed the idea of drawing out a nail into a long pin which could be used to hold a woman's hat or bonnet in place. The hat pins immediately became a popular alternative to the use of bows.

Whitney yearned for a formal education and worked toward this goal until 1792, when he graduated from Yale College. He then took a position as a tutor in the southern state of Georgia. The southern states were in the grip of a severe economic depression at this time because the cotton that was produced could not be adequately "ginned." Ginning involved the removal of seeds from the cotton fibres. The ginning techniques of the day were slow and costly.

The southern plantation owners knew of Whitney's reputation as a mechanical genius and asked him to design a new ginning machine. He protested modestly, "Gentlemen, I don't think I ever saw cotton or cotton seed in my life." Within a few days, however, he had designed a prototype model which could clean cotton as

**Figure 2.5** *Eli Whitney, 1765–1825*

fast as 50 workers. It was President **George Washington** who, on March 14, 1794, signed Whitney's first cotton gin patent. Whitney could not make the machines fast enough to keep up with the demand. When his factory burned down, the cotton farmers of the South began building unlicensed copies. By 1797, over 300 illegal gins were operating. Whitney fought these illegal operators in the law courts to protect his patent rights. In the end, he won $90 000 in damages, but this was almost all used to pay legal expenses. To make matters worse, the patent ran out and the United States Congress refused to grant a renewal. Whitney had saved the cotton farmers of the South, but his genius had brought him little personal profit.

Undaunted, Whitney got a contract from the United States government to manufacture 10 000 muskets. At the time, each musket was made by skilled craftsmen, one at a time. Handcrafted guns were always slightly different, which made them difficult to make and repair. Whitney had two clever ideas. First, he would use machines to manufacture all parts of the muskets. There would be machines for forging, for planing, for grinding, for boring, for polishing, and for any other tasks that could be adapted to machinery. Using this technique, semiskilled machine operators could produce parts which up until that time had been the exclusive work of the most highly skilled craftsmen. It also meant that the same part on different guns would be identical and interchangeable, making repair work faster and cheaper.

Whitney's second idea was to break the manufacturing process down into small steps and give workers responsibility for only one part of the process; thus, there would be workers responsible only for forging, for grinding, or for drilling. The effect of this innovation was to speed up production and to ensure high standards of accuracy. This was very different from the old methods of production where one skilled worker was responsible for making the musket from start to finish.

Whitney's two ideas, the **interchangeability of parts** and the **division of labour**, were two revolutionary ideas that laid the foundation for the techniques of mass production.

Today, Whitney is remembered primarily for the spectacular success of his cotton ginning machine. By 1825, the year of his death, cotton exports from the United States totalled more than $37 million, more than all other exports combined; however, it was Whitney's mass production techniques that truly earned him his status as one of the key figures in the history of American industry.

## PROGRESS CHECK

1. **In 1794, Whitney invented the cotton gin. What was the impact of this invention on the cotton industry?**
2. **What is meant by the term, "mass production"?**
3. **Describe the effect of mass production technology on the creation of small arms. Be sure to refer to two key ideas — interchangeability of parts and division of labour.**

## Transportation

Prior to 1776, the date of the American Declaration of Independence from Britain, over one-third of Britain's ships were built in the American colonies. The American shipbuilding industry was known for its quality and productivity, and was rapidly growing in importance. One American who advanced the technology of shipbuilding was **Robert Fulton**.

**Figure 2.6** *Robert Fulton, 1765–1815*

Fulton was born in 1765 in Pennsylvania. When he was 22 years old, he sailed to London, England, to pursue a career in painting. This proved to be neither financially rewarding nor very stimulating, so Fulton turned his interests to the engineering and design of steamboats and canal systems. Unfortunately, the British had little interest in his steamboats, and found his ideas on canals to be too revolutionary, so Fulton decided to move to Paris and seek his fortune there. Shortly after arriving in Paris, he designed and built a submarine called the *Nautilus*.

As can be seen from Figure 2.7, Fulton's submarine was operated by a hand-driven screw propeller. Fulton actually showed the potential of his new submarine by sinking a number of ships in a demonstration session. He also took the submarine out against a British fleet that was blockading the French coastline, as he was in France at the time when the French and British were at war. The British fleet, however, had been warned, and was able to move out of range of the submarine.

Fulton showed that the submarine could be used as a deadly naval vessel. None of the major military powers of the time chose to develop his submarine, but it is interesting to note that when Jules Verne wrote his famous novel, *20 000 Leagues Under the Sea*, the submarine in the story was called the *Nautilus*. Also, when the United States launched its first atomic-powered submarine in 1955, it was called the *Nautilus*.

Fulton's other interests were to be more rewarding to him. In 1802, he signed an agreement with **Robert Livingston** to build a steamboat. Livingston had been given a monopoly on all steamboat navigation in New York State, but in order to keep the monopoly, he had to have a boat that would average 6.4 km/h between New York and the state capital of Albany. While Livingston was visiting Paris, he offered Fulton an equal share of the profits in his company if he could build a boat to meet the speed requirements. Fulton ordered one of Boulton and Watt's steam engines (see page 11) and installed it in a boat.

The first boat that Fulton tested on the Seine River in Paris sank, but a rebuilt version of the boat achieved a speed of 4.6 km/h. After four more years of hard work, Fulton had a new and faster boat with a more powerful engine, the *Clermont*. In August, 1807, it made the journey from New York to Albany, a distance of 240 km, in 32 hours, achieving an average speed of 7.5 km/h. The monopoly was secured, and Fulton and Livingston prospered.

Fulton's great achievement demonstrated the ability of steamboats to provide successful inland navigation. This helped to open up the country to settlers and to industry. By the time of his death in 1815, Fulton had built 21 steamboats and was recognized as a world leader in steamboat construction.

## PROGRESS CHECK

1. **What two types of water-craft did Fulton help develop?**
2. **In what ways would quick, cheap water transportation help new industries in the United States?**

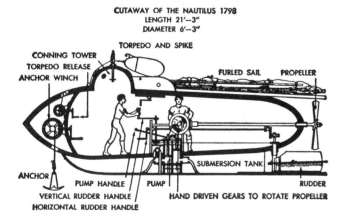

**CUTAWAY OF THE NAUTILUS 1798**
LENGTH 21'–3"
DIAMETER 6'–3"

TORPEDO AND SPIKE

CONNING TOWER
TORPEDO RELEASE
ANCHOR WINCH

FURLED SAIL      PROPELLER

ANCHOR

PUMP HANDLE      PUMP      RUDDER
VERTICAL RUDDER HANDLE      HAND DRIVEN GEARS TO ROTATE PROPELLER
HORIZONTAL RUDDER HANDLE

SUBMERSION TANK

**Figure 2.7** *Fulton's submarine, the* Nautilus, *which he built in 1798.*

# Summary

The efforts of people such as Slater, Wilkinson, Whitney, and Fulton guaranteed that the newly independent United States would move into the industrial age. Their work laid the foundation for an American Industrial Revolution. Slater brought industrial knowledge to the United States; Wilkinson did much to spread the new ideas; Whitney showed how to make interchangeable parts and use the techniques of division of labour; and Fulton improved inland transportation.

Efficient transportation was the key to industrialization. The next major revolution in the industrialization of the United States was the growth of railroads. This is discussed in the next chapter.

# Checking Back

1. Summarize the contributions of key people to the industrialization of the United States by completing a chart similar to the one below.

| NAME | DATE AND PLACE OF BIRTH | KEY INVENTIONS/IDEAS |
|---|---|---|
| Slater | | |
| Wilkinson | | |
| Whitney | SAMPLE ONLY | |
| Fulton | | |

2. "Many great inventions are nothing more than a series of smaller inventions put together." Study some of the major inventions discussed in this chapter to see if this statement is true. You might use a flow chart, time line, or idea web to illustrate your findings.

# Understanding Concepts

3. Explain the concept of mass production by describing how the division of labour and interchangeability of parts changed the small arms industry.

4. Review the contributions of Slater, Wilkinson, Whitney, and Fulton. State in an essay which of these individuals contributed the most to the industrialization of the United States.

# Enrichment

5. Pick a product you would like to manufacture. Using maps of your province, select a site for your factory based on the availability of power, transportation facilities, markets, and raw materials. Prepare a report for your board of directors, explaining your choice. Use an outline map and place important information on it.

6. Issue: Was Sam Slater a traitor to Britain? Although Americans see Sam Slater as a hero, he might be regarded by the British as a traitor because his actions seriously damaged Britain's export trade advantage. Suppose Slater had been caught by a British emigration official. What do you think his trial for illegally trying to emigrate might have been like? Appoint a judge, a jury, a defence lawyer and assistant, plus a prosecution lawyer and assistant. One person should play the role of Sam Slater and another might play the role of his brother, William, who stayed in Britain and might have been unsympathetic to the ideas of his adventuresome brother. The rest of the class can be the jury.

Hold a mock trial, with the defence and prosecution presenting their arguments and calling witnesses, including Sam. When the evidence and arguments are completed, the judge should summarize the discussion and the jury can decide whether Slater was a traitor or not.

# CHAPTER 3

# The Industrial Development of the United States

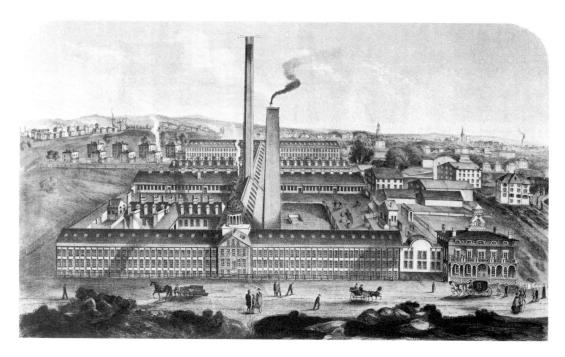

**T**he Industrial Revolution began in Britain and gradually spread to the United States. Emigrants, such as Sam Slater, smuggled out important industrial knowledge to help bring the Industrial Revolution to the New World. By 1820, the foundation of the industrial economy of the United States had been established; however, it would take many years before the United States would become a leading industrial power. This chapter focusses on some of the key industries that triggered the industrial development of the country.

## FOCUS QUESTIONS

1. **How did the United States develop into one of the world's leading industrial powers?**
2. **What industries played a key role in moving the American economy toward maturity?**

## CONCEPTS

| | |
|---|---|
| **trigger industry** | **supply and demand** |
| **change** | **free market economy** |
| **incentives** | **mass consumption** |
| **boom and bust** | |

# Major Industries Trigger Change

When a nation begins to industrialize, one major industry acts as a trigger to cause change in the whole economy. This industry stimulates many other industries so that a wide variety of activities are encouraged. In Britain, the **trigger industry** was the textile industry. It led to the invention of new machinery for harvesting and manufacturing, and caused a huge new demand for power, stimulating the coal mining industry. It also caused an increased demand for transportation as coal had to be moved to factories and finished textiles to markets.

In the United States, the trigger industry was the railroad industry. It gave an enormous boost to the whole American economy. Two other key industries that helped move the American economy toward maturity were the oil and automobile industries.

**Figure 3.1** *Trigger industries set in motion a whole series of changes that led to economic growth.*

# The American Railroad Industry

The wealth and prosperity of a country depends to a large degree on an efficient transportation system. Agricultural products and manufactured goods must be transported to markets and raw materials to mills. People engaging in economic activities need to be able to move from one area to another with relative ease and comfort.

In 1800, the transportation system in the United States was in a primitive state. It was easier to get from New York to Europe by ship than to travel west into the American continent. Transportation inland was by coach, horse, boat, or foot. While canals had become a popular method of transportation in Britain, they were less practical in the United States because the population was much more scattered and distances too great. Still, some form of transportation system was needed to tie the new nation together. **John Stevens**, who had been an officer in George Washington's army in the War of Independence, suggested that a system of railroads might be the answer.

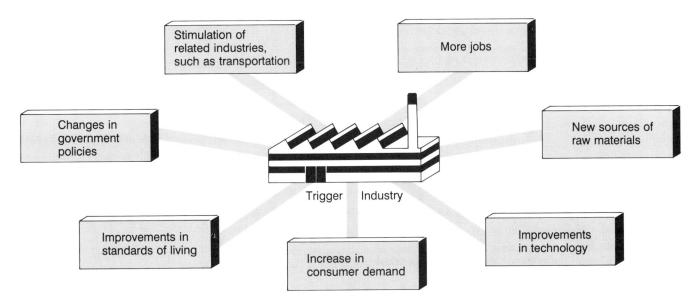

The American railroad industry owes much to the pioneering work of John Stevens. He was born in Manhattan, New York, in 1749. By profession, he was a lawyer, but he was also a mechanical genius who had a strong interest in steam engines. This interest led him to design the first multitubular, marine steam engine in 1788. In order to protect the new design, he lobbied the United States Congress for a patent law, and actually provided a draft copy for such a law. In 1790, President Washington signed the first Patent Act into law. This patent protection stimulated new industrial inventions in the United States because now entrepreneurs were assured that benefits from their ideas would come to them, not others. The accompanying chart of patents shows just how important inventions have been to the economic growth of the United States.

By 1804, Stevens was using a steam-powered boat to travel to and from his island estate on the Hudson River. This boat was designed and built at his own foundry and engineering workshops. It was the first to have underwater screw propellers instead of stern- or side-mounted paddle wheels. In 1809, Stevens' ship the *Phoenix* became the world's first sea-going steamship.

Meanwhile, in Britain, **George Stephenson** had launched the Railway Age with his engine, the *Locomotion*, on the Stockton to Darlington railway line. Stevens imported one of Stephenson's engines, the *John Bull*, and became convinced that the future of transportation was with railroads, an idea years ahead of its time. He argued against developing more canals in favour of a national railway transportation system. Stevens also began working on ways of adapting his steam technology to rail travel. People ridiculed Stevens' ideas, but by 1838, when John Stevens died, the foundation of the great American railroad industry was laid.

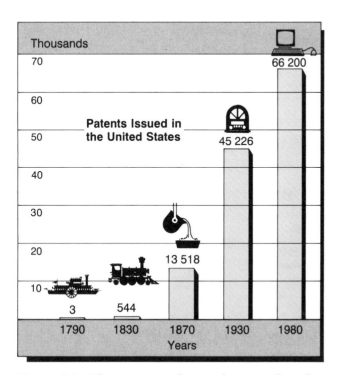

**Figure 3.2** *What are some factors that contributed to this tremendous growth in the number of patents?*

## PROGRESS CHECK

1. **What is a trigger industry?**
2. **Why were canals not the answer to the problem of inland transportation in the United States?**
3. **What solution did Stevens propose to solve the problem of transportation in the United States? What advantages did railroads have over canals?**

## The Railroad Boom

In 1830, there was a famous race between a horse and a locomotive named *Tom Thumb*. **Peter Cooper**, who had built the *Tom Thumb*, staged the race to convince the Baltimore and Ohio Railroad that they should use locomotives rather than horses to pull freight wagons along their rail lines. The locomotive was well in the lead until a belt slipped, allowing the horse to pull ahead and win the race. Despite this setback, the size, power, and reliability of steam locomotives was recognized. In 1831, a locomotive known as the

*Best Friend of Charleston* began making regular runs between Charleston and Hamburg for the South Carolina Canal and Railroad Company. This was the first company in the United States to provide regular passenger and freight service by steam locomotive. By 1835, more than 200 railroad charters had been granted in 11 different states and well over 1500 km of railroad line had been opened.

Extension of the railroads from the settled eastern states into the thinly populated areas in the centre of the continent was expensive and difficult. The government knew that these lands would never be developed without proper transportation facilities. In 1850, the United States Congress decided to help the railroad companies by providing **incentives** in the form of land grants. Federal land was given to state governments who used it to give private railroad companies subsidies. The purpose of these subsidies was to encourage private railway companies to build in less profitable areas. The railroad companies used some of the land grants

**Figure 3.3** *Railroads became a reality in the 1830s. Far-sighted entrepreneurs recognized the value of this form of transportation.*

for the rights of way for the rail lines and sold the rest to help pay construction costs and make a profit. The first railroad built using this form of financial assistance was in Alabama. Once the railroad was built, settlers poured into the area.

The last major hurdle in railroad construction was the building of a line across the country. The Pacific Railroad Act of 1862 gave approval to a plan to build the first transcontinental line. This Act was intended to connect two existing railroads, the Union Pacific and the Central Pacific. The Union Pacific was to build west from Omaha, Nebraska, and the Central Pacific was to go east from its terminus in Sacramento, California. The companies demanded and got large government subsidies because the Union Pacific had to cut through the Rocky Mountains while the Central Pacific had an equally difficult task in crossing the Sierra Nevada Mountains. To

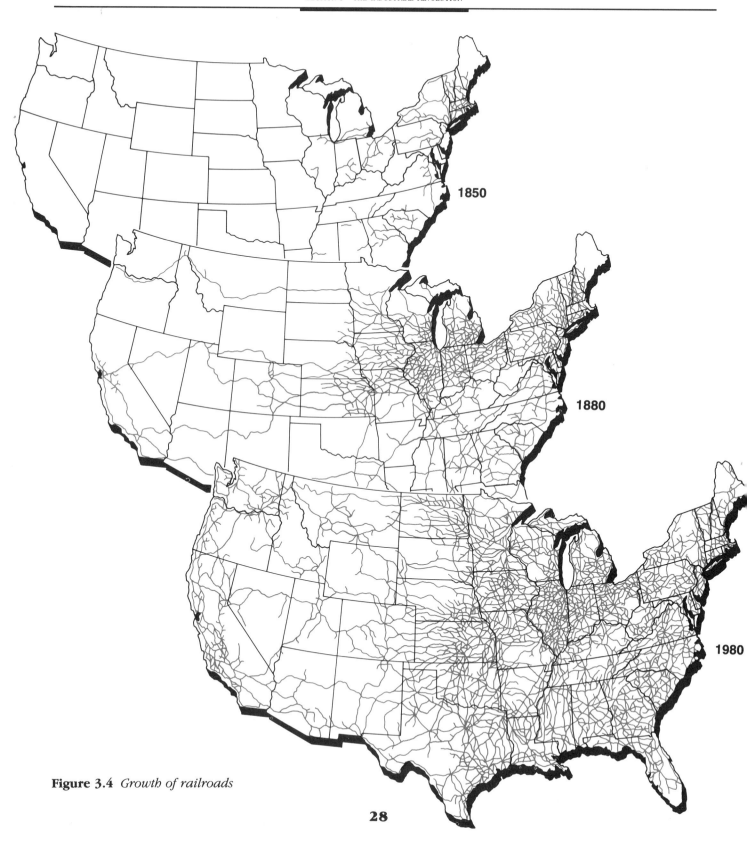

**Figure 3.4** *Growth of railroads*

28

help with the construction, thousands of Chinese labourers, known as **coolies**, were brought into the country by the Central Pacific. The Union Pacific hired European immigrants. The two rail lines finally met on May 10, 1869, at Promontory Point, in the mountains of northern Utah. By the early 1900s, there were four transcontinental lines, and the United States had a vast railroad system crisscrossing the whole country.

**Table 3.1** *Railroads, 1870–1900*

| YEAR | TRACK IN OPERATION (km) | CAPITAL INVESTED (millions) |
|------|------|------|
| 1870 | 84 675 | $ 2 476 |
| 1875 | 118 554 | $ 4 658 |
| 1880 | 149 220 | $ 5 402 |
| 1885 | 205 312 | $ 7 842 |
| 1890 | 266 725 | $10 122 |
| 1895 | 289 051 | $11 007 |
| 1900 | 309 354 | $12 814 |

Table 3.1 shows the size and capital investment in the American railroad industry. This huge investment stimulated industrial growth in a number of related industries. For example, steel was needed for the tracks, and lumber for the railroad ties. Another key development was the creation of hundreds of small towns along the railroads; many towns and cities in the western part of the United States began as railroad stations. The westward expansion and development of the United States was closely tied to the growth of the railroad industry.

## PROGRESS CHECK

1. **In what ways were the railroads important to the development of the interior of the continent?**
2. **When was the first transcontinental railroad completed?**
3. **What are two conclusions you can make about the growth of the railroad industry between 1870 and 1900, based on Table 3.1?**

# The Oil Industry

The oil industry is one of the most important industries in the world today, supplying a relatively cheap, clean source of power for people and industries.

As early as 1750, American colonists knew about oil seepages in various parts of the country, particularly New York State, Pennsylvania, and West Virginia. The uses of oil, however, were limited and there was little **demand** for it. A demand is created when people want to buy a product or service because it fills a need. The famous frontiersman and scout, **Kit Carson**, did find one use for it, however, as axle grease for wagon trains heading west.

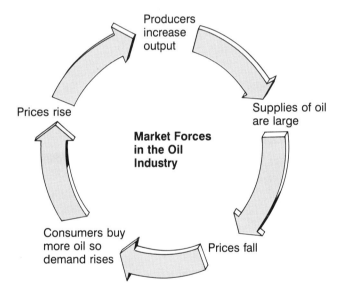

**Figure 3.5** *Using this diagram explain the relationship between supply, demand, and prices.*

The market for oil remained small until the 1840s when **Abraham Gesner**, a Canadian geologist, developed kerosene. This fuel was distilled from oil or coal and was used as a fuel for lamps. By 1854, Gesner had perfected the technology to produce kerosene commercially and the demand for kerosene, and oil, was much greater. Even with this increased demand for oil, however, it was not a prized commodity. Nobody thought of drilling for it because enough appeared from natural seepages (although people digging water wells occasionally found oil instead). But over time, new uses for oil were developed and it became recognized as a valuable natural resource.

In 1857, **George Bissell**, part owner of the Pennsylvania Rock Oil Company, got the idea that there might be oil trapped underground, just like water. If that was true, then oil could be found by drilling wells. Bissell had a great idea, but no money to pay for the drilling of a few test wells. His company was bankrupt. In 1858, he talked to **Edwin Drake** about his ideas. Drake was curious and visited the company properties near Titusville, Pennsylvania. What he saw convinced him to try out Bissell's idea. First, though, he wanted to make sure the venture would be a success. He began by reorganizing Bissell's company and changing the name to the Seneca Oil Company. With the help of people who had experience drilling water wells, Drake began drilling the first oil well in June, 1859. It took most of the summer to punch a hole 20 m deep using a steam-driven drill. The well became known as "Drake's Folly" by the skeptical people of Titusville but, at just over 20 m, they struck oil, and the well became an overnight success.

By the time Drake's well was finished, most of the easy-to-reach surface oil had been used up and the price per barrel was high, about $18. Drake's well was pumping 25 barrels of oil a day and the Seneca Oil Company was making an enormous amount of money. News of this triggered a new kind of "gold" rush, similar to the California gold rush of 1849, except this time it was for "black gold."

The history of the oil industry shows a pattern of **boom** and **bust** that continues today. The wells that were drilled after Drake's discovery began to produce so much oil that the market was flooded and the price dropped to only 10

cents a barrel within three years. The low price, however, was only one of a great many problems facing the infant oil industry. There were immediate technical problems of storing, transporting, and refining oil.

At first, oil was stored in the ground in wooden reservoirs. These reservoirs were later made of cement. Eventually, the oil companies began building the huge, above-ground steel tanks we see today.

**Figure 3.6** *Edwin Drake drilled the first oil well in the United States in 1859, but the* world's *first oil well was drilled in Ontario by James Williams in 1858 to a depth of 15 m.*

Transportation was a difficult problem because oil was often discovered in remote areas. It had to be transported to a refinery for processing. The first solution was to use teamsters to haul the oil in large horse-drawn wagons, but this proved to be slow and costly. The railroads offered a better solution. Trains hauled the oil in barrels stacked on flat railroad cars. Later, the flat cars were replaced with specially built wooden tank cars and then steel tank cars. The best solution to the problem of moving huge amounts of oil came with the development of pipelines. In time, North America was crisscrossed with a network of pipelines covering thousands of kilometres.

**Figure 3.7** *An oil field in Texas. How did such mismanagement of resources hurt the oil industry?*

The refining process presented the biggest challenge. At first, kerosene was the main product of the refining process. In making kerosene, one of the nuisance by-products was gasoline. Since internal combustion engines were not developed at the time, there was no demand for gasoline and it was often simply dumped into nearby rivers and creeks. This state of affairs lasted until about 1900. At that time, a new invention, the electric light bulb, began to replace the kerosene lamp. Electricity was much safer and provided a brighter, more even source of light, so the demand for kerosene began to drop. Also, the automobile was becoming popular as a means of transportation, creating a whole new market for gasoline. Refining methods at this time were primitive, so it took 100 barrels of crude oil to produce just 11 barrels of gasoline. In 1913, the new refining process of thermal cracking was developed; within five years, refineries had more than doubled the amount of gasoline that could be produced from a given amount of oil. In addition, many new products were being discovered using oil as the raw material.

The demand for oil and gasoline products grew enormously during World War I (1914–1918) and World War II (1939–1945). Tanks, ships, and airplanes all used huge quantities of these products. The **petrochemical industry** expanded and new refining processes, such as catalytic cracking, produced gasolines with higher octanes suitable for high-performance cars and aviation fuel.

What were the key ingredients that contributed to the growth of the oil industry? They were the same ingredients that we have seen all along as being important to the growth of any new industry—ideas, labour, and capital. In the oil industry, ideas were supplied by George Bissell and others who decided to look for oil underground. Those people who drilled oil wells and moved the oil to market supplied the labour. Capital was provided by investors who took risks to back the Seneca Oil Company and similar companies involved in the oil industry.

**Table 3.2** *Oil Production in the United States*

| YEAR | PRODUCTION (BARRELS) |
| --- | --- |
| 1859 | 2 000 |
| 1860 | 250 000 |
| 1900 | 64 000 000 |
| 1980s | 3 000 000 000 |

## PROGRESS CHECK

1. **Where was the first oil found and how was it used?**
2. **What was kerosene used for? How did it affect the oil industry?**
3. **Which oil company drilled the first oil well in the United States? Where was it drilled?**
4. **Describe how the oil industry solved the following problems:**
    (a) **storage**
    (b) **transportation**
    (c) **refining.**

## John D. Rockefeller and the Oil Industry

Important developments in the early days of the oil industry revolved around the famous industrialist, **John D. Rockefeller**. Rockefeller, the son of a peddler, entered the oil business when he was only 23 years old, with profits from his grain-selling business. In 1870, he started the Standard Oil Company of Ohio, a firm that eventually became the first billion-dollar corporation. Rockefeller bought or built oil wells, refineries, pipelines, and even retail sales outlets, controlling everything from the production of crude oil to the sale of the finished product. Gaining complete control of an industry in this fashion became known as **vertical integration**.

Rockefeller's greatest problems stemmed from the nature of the oil industry itself. The industry was subject to the boom and bust cycles of a free market. Sometimes the price of a barrel of oil dropped to less than that of a barrel of water.

Supply and demand are two key factors that control the price of any commodity in a free market economy. When demand is high, the price goes up, but when demand is low, the price drops. Prices also drop when supply is too great for the demand. Rockefeller decided to do something to control erratic price swings. Between 1870 and 1882, he and his business partners bought most of the oil refineries in Cleveland, Ohio, and in a number of other cities. In this way, he could control the supply of oil to keep prices high enough to make a good profit. Control of the oil industry was formalized with the creation of the Standard Oil Trust in 1882. Rockefeller and the members of the Trust controlled about 90 percent of the United States oil refining industry at that time.

Such control is known as **horizontal integration** of an industry.

**Figure 3.8**
*John D. Rockefeller*

32

**Table 3.3** *"Boom–bust" Oil Prices For Selected Years*

| YEAR | PRICE PER BARREL ($US) |
|------|------------------------|
| 1859 | $18.00 |
| 1860 | $ .10 |
| 1973 | $ 2.80 |
| 1974 | $10.84 |
| 1982 | $34.00 |
| 1986 | $10.00 |
| 1989 | $20.00 |

The Trust's activities were bitterly criticized by many people. When businesses combine to form trusts, cartels, or trade associations, they can make agreements to fix high prices on their goods or services. Agreements of this kind destroy competition among businesses and hurt consumers. Without competition, the market economy is no longer "free." Rockefeller, a great promoter of a free market economy, was bending the rules for personal gain.

To restore competition to the oil industry, the United States government passed a series of laws. The first was the Sherman Antitrust Act of 1890 which made it illegal to form combinations or groups which restrain trade. The Act also made it illegal to create a **monopoly** where only one firm could control a whole industry. Other antitrust laws have been passed since that time in the United States, Canada, and most other industrialized countries.

The Sherman Antitrust Act was used by the state of Ohio to dissolve the Rockefeller Trust. But Rockefeller was not beaten. He simply went to the state of New Jersey and formed a new company called Standard Oil of New Jersey. New Jersey allowed firms to hold shares in other companies outside the state. Standard Oil of New Jersey bought shares in all the other companies of the old Trust and regained control of the oil industry; however, new antitrust action, launched in 1906 by President **Theodore Roosevelt**, dealt a tremendous blow to Standard Oil. Evidence showed that the company had made huge profits—nearly $1 billion—in a quarter of a century. It took five years before the complex court action was resolved. Finally, in 1911, the court decided against Standard Oil and ordered the firm to sell all of its subsidiaries.

One of the lessons learned from the Rockefeller Trust monopoly was the need for government intervention to ensure free market conditions. Ideally, in a free market economy, governments stay out of the way of business, yet the Trust showed that it was possible for a business to form a monopoly and control an industry. From this, one can clearly see that laws are sometimes needed to prevent such monopolies. The key issue is: To what extent should the government interfere with the free market economy of the United States? This question is examined in later chapters of this book and, as you might expect, is very difficult to answer.

Many of the old Standard Oil firms have since become some of the largest companies in the world. These firms include Exxon, Mobil, Amoco, Chevron, and Atlantic Richfield. Exxon, the new name for Standard Oil, is still the largest oil company in the world.

## PROGRESS CHECK

1. **What is meant by vertical and horizontal integration?**
2. **Why did Rockefeller form the Standard Oil Trust? What was the effect of the Trust?**
3. **What techniques did the government of the United States use to break up the oil monopoly held by Rockefeller?**
4. **Issue: Was the government right to pass laws to break up the Standard Oil Trust? Record points for both sides of this issue. After you have looked at both viewpoints, decide which side you support. Write a position statement on the question, listing reasons for your opinion.**

# Henry Ford and the American Automobile Industry

**Henry Ford** was an American automobile manufacturer who pioneered assembly line techniques to mass produce cars. He is another example of an industrialist who took a good idea and developed it. His work had a great impact on the growth of American industry.

Henry Ford was born in 1863 on a farm near Dearborn, Michigan. He trained as a machinist and built his first gasoline engine in 1893.

**Figure 3.9** *Henry Ford's first car had no steering wheel, just a tiller. It was really no more than a box on wheels with only one seat; however, this crude car still runs today!*

Contrary to popular opinion, Ford did not invent the automobile. People had been experimenting with self-propelled vehicles since Watt developed the steam engine. **Carl Benz**, a German, is generally credited with inventing the first automobile powered by a gasoline engine. He patented his automobile on January 29, 1886. By the early 1890s, the idea of a gasoline-powered automobile had crossed the Atlantic and, in 1896, Ford developed his own automobile with a gasoline motor.

Ford established his Ford Motor Company in 1903. Five years later, he introduced his most famous car of all, the Ford "Model T," or Tin Lizzie as it came to be called. The Model T combined speed (up to 70 km/h) with reliable performance and low cost.

The Model T was like no other automobile of the day. Prior to its invention, cars had been built in small numbers for rich people. The original price of the Model T was a mere $850, within the range of average people. Ford was able to achieve this exceptionally low price by making use of **assembly line methods** and **mass production techniques**. Indeed, in 1914, he began offering the Model T only in black because other colours of paint would not dry fast enough to keep pace with the speed of the assembly line. He also pursued vertical integration within his company, gaining control of firms manufacturing component parts and raw materials for his automobiles.

Because the Model T was offered at such a low price, Ford sold more than 15 million vehicles between 1908 and 1927. He kept the design of the Model T largely unchanged over the years, which allowed him to cut the cost of the car even more. He had the price down to $260 by 1923, the peak production year for Model Ts (two million were produced). Ford made the United States the number one automobile producer in the world. By 1927, the company was producing 81 percent of all automobiles built anywhere in the world. That same year, the United States manufactured 3.5 million automobiles while Britain, the second largest producer, built only 212 000 automobiles.

Automobile manufacturing is important in an economy because it uses the products of many other industries. Think about some of the raw materials that are used in manufacturing automobiles. Steel and rubber are two obvious examples. The multitude of companies that supply parts and services to the car manufacturers like the Ford Motor Company provide hundreds of thousands of jobs in North America.

By making automobiles affordable for ordinary working people, Henry Ford ushered in the age of **high mass consumption**. Consumer spending stimulated many businesses, which led to more jobs, which led to greater consumer spending, and so on. The automobile industry helped make the United States one of the world's leading industrial powers. This is a position it still holds today although this leadership is now being challenged by Japan.

One character trait of Henry Ford made him quite different from other industrialists of his day. He was particularly concerned about his workers. On January 5, 1914, he astounded the business community by reducing the working day from

**Figure 3.10** *Model Ts coming off an assembly line in Highland Park, Michigan, in 1914*

nine to eight hours and increasing the wages of his 13 000 employees to $5 per day. Until that time, unskilled workers had received $1 and skilled workers $2.50 a day. He also announced a profit-sharing plan for his employees. This news made the headlines in almost every major newspaper. It represented a new era in **industrial relations** and made automobile workers one of the highest paid groups in the American economy. Ford had good reason for taking these steps. He recognized that higher wages for auto workers would stimulate higher wages in other industries. This would mean greater purchasing power for American workers, and greater purchasing power would mean that he could sell more of his automobiles. The so-called "Ford idea" quickly spread to other industries and consumer spending began to mushroom.

Henry Ford was both a **pacifist** and **philanthropist**. He opposed the entry of the United States into both world wars, although once the U.S. was committed, he turned his factories over to the manufacture of war materials. Ford boasted during World War II that his Willow Run, Michigan, plant turned out a bomber an hour. Ford and his son, Edsel, established the Ford Foundation to which they donated large amounts of money. This was a philanthropic foundation which gave money to organizations concerned with poverty, human rights and justice, education, culture, international affairs, and population issues. This philanthropic concern of many American industries is often overlooked in the total picture of the effect of industry on the lives of people.

## PROGRESS CHECK

1. **Who invented the first gasoline-powered car? When was it invented?**
2. **Why was Ford able to sell so many Model Ts?**
3. **Why was Ford willing to pay his workers twice the average wage?**

# Summary

The industrial development of the United States was triggered by several key activities in the railroad, oil, and automobile industries. These industries developed through the hard work of individual entrepreneurs such as John Stevens, Edwin Drake, John D. Rockefeller, and Henry Ford. Through their efforts and ideas, the lives of all Americans changed. In the process, they propelled the United States into the 20th century as a leading industrial power.

# Checking Back

1. In what ways did the railroad industry trigger the development of the United States economy?
2. Pick one of the industrialists studied in this chapter and outline the impact of his work on the North American economy and society. How were the lives of people changed? What are some of the long-term effects of that person's work?
3. What is meant by the terms "market", "supply", and "demand"? Write a paragraph stating how the oil market was affected by the invention of kerosene. How was the supply of oil affected when Edwin Drake succeeded in drilling an oil well?

| TIME LINE |
|---|
| **1800** |
| **1825** —John Stevens develops the first U.S. railroad locomotive |
| **1831** —The South Carolina Canal and Railroad Company opens |
| **1850** |
| **1850** —The U.S. Congress provides the first federal land grants to encourage the development of American railroads |

**1859** — Edwin Drake drills well at Titusville, Pa.
**1869** — The Central Pacific and Union Pacific
— the world's first transcontinental line
— is completed
**1896** — Henry Ford and others introduce their
gasoline-powered automobiles
**1900**
**1908** — Ford introduces the Model T
**1913** — The thermal cracking process is invented

# Understanding Concepts

4. Review the information about Henry Ford and John Rockefeller and answer these questions about each individual:
   (a) What new ideas did he develop?
   (b) How did the industry change because of these ideas?
   (c) What impact did the changes make on the lives of people?
   (d) What was the lasting contribution to society?
   (e) What is your opinion of the individual?
5. Write an essay on the topic, "John D. Rockefeller: Hero or Villain?".

# Enrichment

6. Compare the building of the first transcontinental railroad in the United States to the building of the Canadian Pacific Railroad in Canada. Identify the similarities and differences. What was the role of the government in each case? Use an illustrated time line to display this information.
7. Analyze and evaluate the antitrust laws in the United States to determine how effective they are in breaking up monopolies. Select a good article on the subject from a periodical in a library (or information network system) and explain why you agree or disagree with the article.

8. Investigate some current developments in the oil industry. How does the oil industry now solve problems of storage, transportation, and refining?
9. Compare the Rockefeller Trust to the Organization of Petroleum Exporting Countries (OPEC). How do the goals, methods, and results compare?
10. Issue: Should governments give subsidies to private railroad companies to encourage development in remote areas? Government support for private companies is a very difficult political issue. Here are a few arguments for and against the issue. Can you think of others?

**SOME ARGUMENTS FOR SUBSIDIES**
- Private businesses operate to make a profit, so they will never build in unprofitable areas unless forced to do so by law, or persuaded by incentives, such as land grants.
- People in remote areas have a right to decent transportation. If the private companies will not build, then the government must use incentives to ensure that they do.
- This is a good investment for the country in the long term.

**SOME ARGUMENTS AGAINST SUBSIDIES**
- Government and private business should not mix.
- Governments should not waste tax dollars on a few people who live in remote areas.
- If a project does not make economic sense, it should not be built.

Give your position on this issue in a one-page position paper. Make sure you back up your opinions with good reasons.

# Physical and Economic Geography of the United States

Section I traced the historical development of the American industrial economy from its roots in the British Industrial Revolution. Key industries were studied to show how the United States changed from a simple agricultural society into one of the world's most important industrialized nations. This historical background provides an understanding of the economy, but our knowledge would be incomplete without a close examination of the geography of the United States. Geography helps us to understand the decisions made to locate industries in certain places. The geography of a country is shaped by natural forces while the history of a country is created by people.

Chapters 4 and 5 deal with the physical and human geography of the United States. Both these aspects influence the location and distribution of industry. Chapter 6 shows how the relationships among business, government, and labour have also affected the industrial development of the United States.

## SECTION II

**Chapter 4:** Physical Geography and Resources
**Chapter 5:** Geography, People, and Industry
**Chapter 6:** Government, Business and Labour

As you study this section of the book, keep these questions in mind:

- How does the physical geography of the United States affect the distribution of primary industries?
- What factors influence the location and distribution of secondary and tertiary industries?
- What were the roles of government, labour, and industry in the development of the American economy?

# CHAPTER 4

# *Physical Geography and Resources*

The physical geography of the United States includes the shape of the land, the distribution of rocks and minerals, the distribution of soils and vegetation, the climate, and the distribution of ocean currents. All of these features have played a role in influencing the growth and distribution of the country's **primary industries**. Primary industries are based on the extraction of natural resources found in nature, and include the mining and oil industries, forestry, farming, and fishing.

The physical geography of a country determines the kind of primary industries that will be successful. If we know about rainfall and temperatures, we can tell if certain crops or trees will grow in an area. A country that has large forests can support a lumber industry. If there are rich soils for growing crops, a strong farming industry may develop. An understanding of the **geology** of a country will be useful in predicting the best areas for mining. Knowledge about the ocean currents and the shape of the seabed will be important for fishing. Understanding the physical geography of the United States is important in helping us to explain the distribution of primary industries.

## FOCUS QUESTIONS

1. **What are the major landscape regions of the United States?**
2. **What natural resources are found in the United States?**
3. **What is the relationship between natural resources and primary industries?**

## CONCEPTS

primary industries    glaciation
region    vegetation
natural resources    climatic influences

# The Major Landscapes of the United States

The United States is very rich in natural resources and has a variety of landscapes. Ten major **landscape regions** are identified on the map in Figure 4.1. A region is an area that has common characteristics. We can define regions according to a number of factors—political characteristics, economic factors, social considerations, and so on. In this chapter, regions will be based on common physical characteristics of the land. The landscape regions are:

The Appalachian Mountains
The Gulf-Atlantic Coastal Lowlands and Piedmont
The Interior and Great Plains
The Interior Highlands
The Rocky Mountains
The Intermontane Basins and Plateaus
The Pacific Ranges and Coastal Lowlands
The Canadian Shield
The Arctic Coastal Plain
The Volcanic Islands of Hawaii

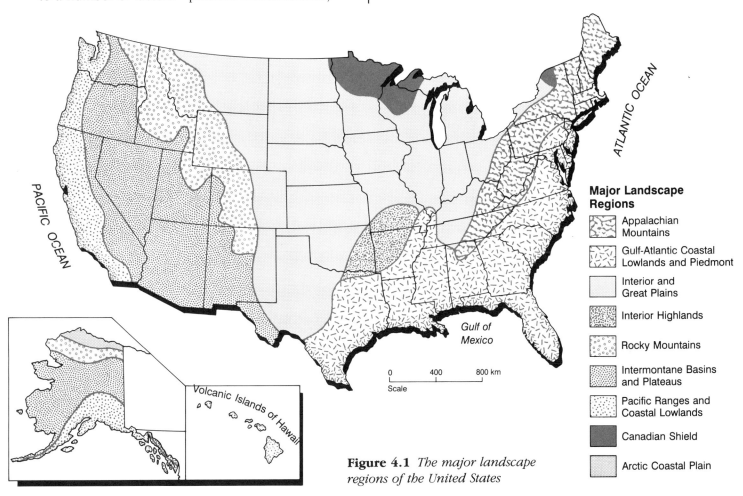

**Major Landscape Regions**

- Appalachian Mountains
- Gulf-Atlantic Coastal Lowlands and Piedmont
- Interior and Great Plains
- Interior Highlands
- Rocky Mountains
- Intermontane Basins and Plateaus
- Pacific Ranges and Coastal Lowlands
- Canadian Shield
- Arctic Coastal Plain

**Figure 4.1** *The major landscape regions of the United States*

# The Appalachian Mountains

| KEY FEATURES | NATURAL RESOURCES | PRIMARY INDUSTRIES |
|---|---|---|
| Low mountains Rivers Rocky, with thin soils | Rugged forests Some coal, oil, iron ore | Lumber Mining |

This area includes the ruggedly beautiful Blue Ridge Mountains and several famous rivers, including the Delaware, Hudson, Potomac, and Susquehanna. The outstanding natural beauty of the Appalachians has made it an important area for tourism. Highways and railroads are built along the gaps cut through the mountains by rivers. In the plateau areas adjacent to the mountains are rich deposits of coal, oil, and iron ore. The area is important for mining, but generally not for farming since the soil is poor and thin.

# The Gulf-Atlantic Coastal Lowlands and Piedmont

| KEY FEATURES | NATURAL RESOURCES | PRIMARY INDUSTRIES |
|---|---|---|
| Low-lying, flat land Coastal plains | Rich soil Oil, natural gas | Agriculture, especially tobacco, vegetables, cotton |

Many of the original Thirteen Colonies are located in this large area. The rich soils make it suitable for farming. Tobacco and cotton are two of the most important cash crops, but vegetables, citrus fruits, and peanuts are also grown in large quantities. In the Gulf Coastal Plain, the Mississippi and other rivers regularly flood the land, depositing a rich, fertile soil known as an **alluvial soil**. This area also contains underground

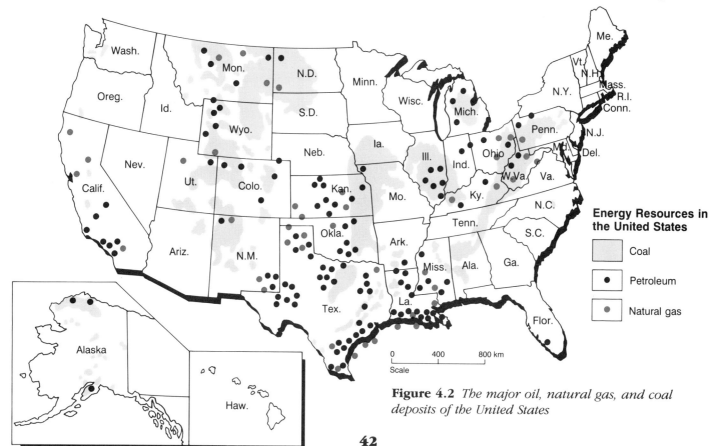

**Figure 4.2** *The major oil, natural gas, and coal deposits of the United States*

rock formations which have rich deposits of oil and natural gas. The oil and gas industry is very important to the economy of the Gulf area.

## The Interior and Great Plains

| KEY FEATURES | NATURAL RESOURCES | PRIMARY INDUSTRIES |
|---|---|---|
| Flat land Effects of glaciation | Forests Rich soils Gas, oil, coal, iron ore | Agriculture, including cereal crops, animal farming |

This region also has a varied geography and can be divided into two parts—the Interior Plains in the East and the Great Plains in the West. During the ice ages, the land was covered by **glaciers**. In parts of the North, including portions of Minnesota, Michigan, and Wisconsin, the glaciers

stripped away much of the topsoil. Today, these northern areas support forests that thrive in spite of the poor, thin soils. Further to the South, in parts of Illinois, Indiana, Iowa, and Ohio, the land is flat and covered by thick topsoils deposited by the glaciers. This part of the region is ideal for farming as the drier climate is good for growing animal feed and cereal crops. The Plains also have significant deposits of oil, natural gas, coal, iron ore, and other metals. This area is the centre of a number of key primary industries.

## The Interior Highlands

| KEY FEATURES | NATURAL RESOURCES | PRIMARY INDUSTRIES |
|---|---|---|
| Hills and valleys | Minerals, coal, metals | Mining |

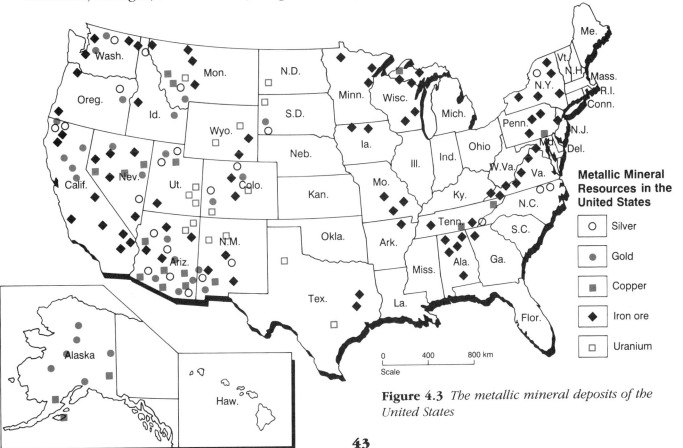

**Figure 4.3** *The metallic mineral deposits of the United States*

This area includes the Ozark Plateau and the Ouachita Highlands. The Interior Highlands are located between the Coastal Lowlands and the Interior Plains. Apart from the fertile river valleys, this is a poor area for farming because of the thin, relatively infertile soils. This small area does have important deposits of coal, iron ore, and other minerals.

## The Rocky Mountains

| KEY FEATURES | NATURAL RESOURCES | PRIMARY INDUSTRIES |
|---|---|---|
| Mountains River valleys Meadows | Oil, natural gas, metals Fertile valley soils | Mining Beef, dairy, and mixed farming |

This area contains part of the largest mountain chain in North America. The Rocky Mountains stretch from Alaska in the North, through Canada to the northern part of New Mexico. The **continental divide** runs through the mountains, with the rivers west of the divide flowing down to the Pacific and those east flowing to the Atlantic. This is an area of great natural beauty, and tourism thrives. There is a wide variety of vegetation up to the **tree line**, above which trees do not grow because of the colder temperatures at high altitudes.

The Rocky Mountains have some of the most important natural resources in the United States, including **hydrocarbons** (oil and natural gas) and metals, such as copper, gold, lead, silver, and zinc. Parts of this area support agriculture. The mountain meadows have beef and dairy farming, and the more fertile valleys are used for growing crops.

This area played a significant role in the historical development of the United States because it formed a barrier to transportation. The communities on the Pacific Coast were poorly linked to the rest of the United States until the first transcontinental railroad broke through the Rocky Mountains.

## The Intermontane Basins and Plateaus

| KEY FEATURES | NATURAL RESOURCES | PRIMARY INDUSTRIES |
|---|---|---|
| Deserts Great Salt Lake Grand Canyon | Fertile river valleys | Livestock farming Irrigated farming |

This region stretches from the Mexican border in the South almost all the way to the Canadian border. For the most part, it lies west of the Rocky Mountains. The region contains some of the driest deserts in the country. There are many unusual landforms in this area, including the

magnificent gorge of the Grand Canyon of the Colorado River, and Death Valley in California. Parts of Death Valley lie almost 90 m below sea level. Great Salt Lake, located in the Great Basin area of Utah, is so salty that swimmers will not sink in it. Nearby is the Great Salt Lake Desert which is an enormous area of very smooth, hard, salt deposits. It was used to set many of the world's land speed records.

This region has large sheep and cattle ranches. Crops are grown on irrigated land in the fertile valleys, with cotton and sugar beet crops grown in the southern states.

**Figure 4.4** *The Grand Canyon formed by the erosion of the Colorado River over millions of years.*

## The Pacific Ranges and Coastal Lowlands

| KEY FEATURES | NATURAL RESOURCES | PRIMARY INDUSTRIES |
|---|---|---|
| Mountains, coastal ranges | Rich soils | Fishing<br>Grape growing<br>Market gardening |

The eastern boundary of this region is formed by the Cascade Mountains in the North and by the Sierra Nevada Mountains in the South. The Cascade Mountains were formed by volcanic activity and two of the peaks are still active volcanos — Lassen Peak in California and Mount St. Helen's in the state of Washington. Mount St. Helen's had a devastating eruption in 1980.

There are broad, fertile valleys to the west of the mountains, and even further west lie the Coast Ranges. In some places, these ranges reach right to the coast, creating some magnificent scenery. Elsewhere, the mountains lie behind sandy plains. This area includes deep bays cut into the coastline, Puget Sound and San Francisco Bay being examples. These bays have encouraged

**Figure 4.5** *The Mount St. Helen's eruption in 1980*

the development of a wide variety of marine-based industries and activities.

The geology of the region is important in another respect, for it is through these Coast Ranges that the **San Andreas Fault** runs. This fault is a crack or break in the earth's crust that has been responsible for numerous earthquakes, including the one which devastated San Francisco in 1906. It is widely predicted that another major earthquake will occur in the next 50 years.

The coastal region is also known for its **market gardening**, which is the growing of fruit and vegetables. The produce grown in this area is shipped all over the United States and to parts of western Canada. Grapes are grown for fresh or dried produce or for wine. Wine making has grown to become a major industry.

## The Canadian Shield

| KEY FEATURES | NATURAL RESOURCES | PRIMARY INDUSTRIES |
|---|---|---|
| Glaciated rock formations Small lakes | Iron ore Forests | Mining Lumber |

The Canadian Shield dips down into the United States near the Great Lakes. It is composed of very old, hard, crystalline rocks. The natural drainage patterns of the land were destroyed by continental ice sheets that scraped out numerous hollows in the rock and resulted in the creation of thousands of lakes. In fact, the central and northern part of Minnesota is known as "The Land of 10 000 Lakes." The ice sheets were over 1.5 km thick, and their massive weight depressed the surface of the land. As the ice melted, the land rose again, and in some areas is still rising, by a process known as **isostatic rebound**.

The Shield rocks are different from those in other parts of the United States. They contain some rich deposits of iron ore that have been mined to support the huge steel industry in the Pittsburgh area.

## The Arctic Coastal Plain

| KEY FEATURES | NATURAL RESOURCES | PRIMARY INDUSTRIES |
|---|---|---|
| Tundra (treeless plain) Rugged coastline | Oil Fish | Oil Fishing |

Alaska contains parts of many of the landforms found in the lower 48 states. The Pacific Ranges, the Intermontane Basins and Plateaus, and the Rocky Mountains, all extend into Alaska. The Arctic Coastal Plain on Alaska's northern coastline, though, is very different from the southern plains because of the extremely cold climate. This plain is a grassy, treeless area, part of the **tundra**. The soil is permanently frozen and is known as **permafrost**. Important mineral deposits, including oil at Prudhoe Bay, are located on the Arctic Coastal Plain. Oil from the region is transported to the port of Valdez on the southern coast of Alaska by the $8 billion Trans-Alaska Pipeline, which was completed in 1977.

## The Volcanic Islands of Hawaii

| KEY FEATURES | NATURAL RESOURCES | PRIMARY INDUSTRIES |
|---|---|---|
| Volcanic features Sandy beaches Natural harbours | Fertile soils Fish | Sugar cane Pineapple farming |

The Volcanic Islands of Hawaii are distinctive because of their mountains and their location about 4000 km southwest of the United States mainland. The islands are at a latitude of about 20°N and have a tropical climate. The naturally hot temperatures are cooled by Pacific winds, giving the islands an ideal climate. The climate and rich, volcanic soils in the valleys have combined to make the island a major centre for the growing of sugar cane and pineapples. Some cattle farming and mixed farming also occur.

Their geographic location in the Pacific Ocean also makes these islands important for military reasons. The United States has maintained a major naval base on the island of Oahu at Pearl Harbour since 1887.

## PROGRESS CHECK

1. **What is a natural resource? What is a primary industry? List three examples of natural resources and primary industries.**
2. **Identify landscape regions that contain the following natural resources:**
   **(a) rich soil      (c) iron ore**
   **(b) fish           (d) oil and natural gas.**
3. **Based on the descriptions of the ten landscape regions, which three areas do you think would be the most thinly populated? Briefly explain the reasons for your choices.**

# Temperature, Precipitation, and Vegetation

The ten landscape regions of the United States contain a wide variety of physical characteristics. Landforms are obviously different, but we can also look at other aspects of physical geography, such as **temperature**, **precipitation**, and **vegetation**.

## Temperature

Geographers studying climate usually look at two temperatures in order to get an accurate picture of an area's climate. These two temperatures are the averages for the months of January and July. Figure 4.6 shows the average January temperatures across the United States. Three factors influence the patterns that appear on the map.

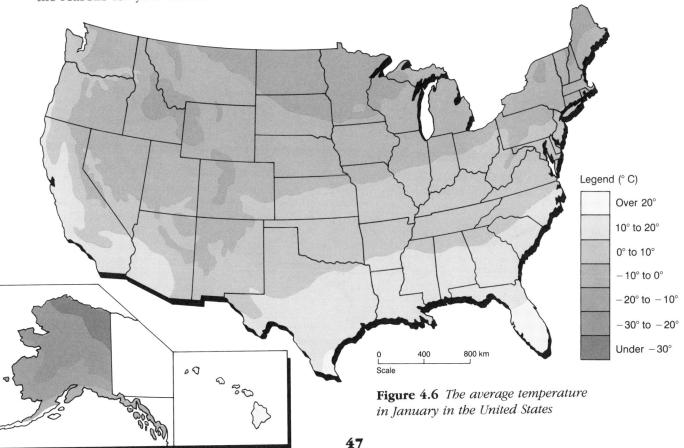

Legend (° C)

Over 20°
10° to 20°
0° to 10°
−10° to 0°
−20° to −10°
−30° to −20°
Under −30°

0      400      800 km
Scale

**Figure 4.6** *The average temperature in January in the United States*

1. **Distance from the equator**—Places in southern parts of the country are much warmer than places with more northern latitudes. This is because the sun's rays shine more directly closer to the equator than farther north. The more direct rays have a greater heating ability, so the climate is warmer.

2. **Distance from the ocean**—Minneapolis is colder than Boston despite the fact that both cities are at roughly the same latitude. This phenomenon occurs because oceans have a moderating influence on nearby land climates. In winter, oceans tend to retain heat much more than the land, and they release this heat more slowly; thus, the land near an ocean benefits from the heat retained in the water.

3. **Altitude**—Most of the heat from the sun arrives in the form of long-wave radiation which heats the ground, but not the atmosphere. The heat in the air comes from the warmed surface of the earth, so the air closer to the ground tends to be warmer. As altitude increases, air temperatures decrease. The decline in air temperature is known as the **lapse rate**.

The coldest parts of the lower 48 states in January are in the extreme North at some distance from the oceans. Minneapolis, for example, has an average January temperature just below −9°C. Also very cold are the high Rocky Mountains. The warmest January temperatures are recorded in the extreme South near oceans.

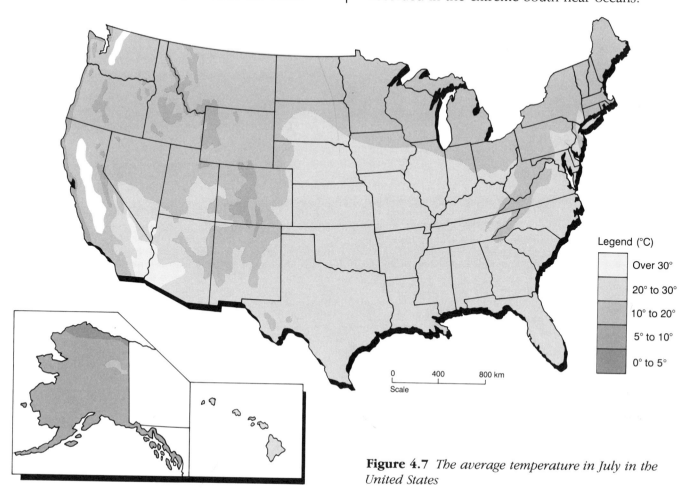

Legend (°C)

Over 30°
20° to 30°
10° to 20°
5° to 10°
0° to 5°

0    400    800 km
Scale

**Figure 4.7** *The average temperature in July in the United States*

Florida, Texas, and southern California are examples of such locations.

Figure 4.7 shows the average July temperatures. The two factors of distance to the equator and altitude also influence the average temperatures in July. The oceans, however, act as a cooling influence in July, especially on the West Coast. The water heats up more slowly than surrounding land masses and this moderates the high summer temperatures. The hottest places are found in southern locations in the interior of the continent. The city of Phoenix, Arizona, for example, has an average July temperature of over 32°C. In the northern states, average

temperatures are 16°C to 24°C, and parts of the Rocky Mountains are even cooler, with averages from 7°C to 16°C.

## Precipitation

Figure 4.8 shows the average annual precipitation for the United States. Precipitation includes all forms of moisture falling on the surface of the earth. On precipitation maps, lines joining places with the same average annual precipitation are known as **isohyets**. Isohyets are a specific type of **isoline**, which is a term referring to any line on a map joining points with equal values.

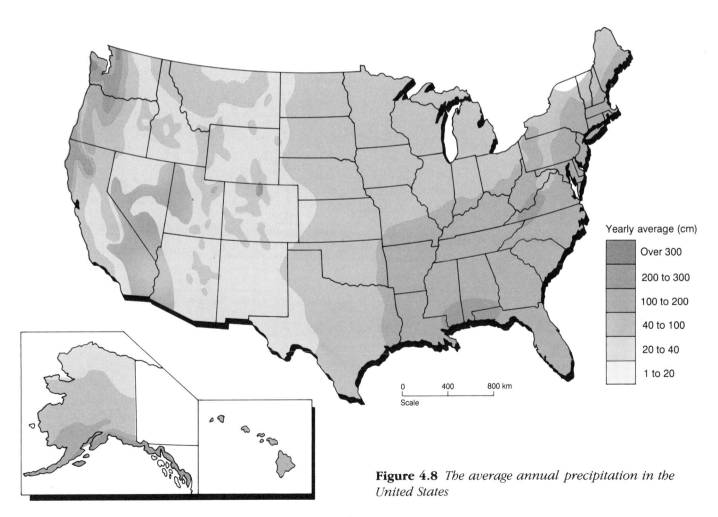

Yearly average (cm)

Over 300
200 to 300
100 to 200
40 to 100
20 to 40
1 to 20

0    400    800 km
Scale

**Figure 4.8** *The average annual precipitation in the United States*

## Vegetation

The type of vegetation which grows in a particular region depends upon the rainfall, temperature, and the physical relief of the landscape. It is a reflection of all the other aspects of the physical geography of an area. Figure 4.9 shows the major types of vegetation in the United States. Compare this map to the maps of precipitation and rainfall to identify similarities in patterns.

### PROGRESS CHECK

1. **What are three factors that will determine how warm or cold a place will be?**
2. **Minneapolis is at about the same latitude as Boston, yet their average temperatures are quite different. Explain why.**
3. **What is meant by the terms "isoline" and "isohyet"?**
4. **How will temperature and precipitation affect the vegetation of an area?**

## Summary

The environment must be seen as a whole. The land is shaped by forces in nature. Climate is determined by factors such as distance from the equator, proximity to oceans, and altitude. These factors interact to determine the kinds of vegetation that grow in a region.

## Checking Back

1. Construct a chart similar to the one shown to record information about the landscape regions of the United States. Fill in the chart using the information in this chapter.

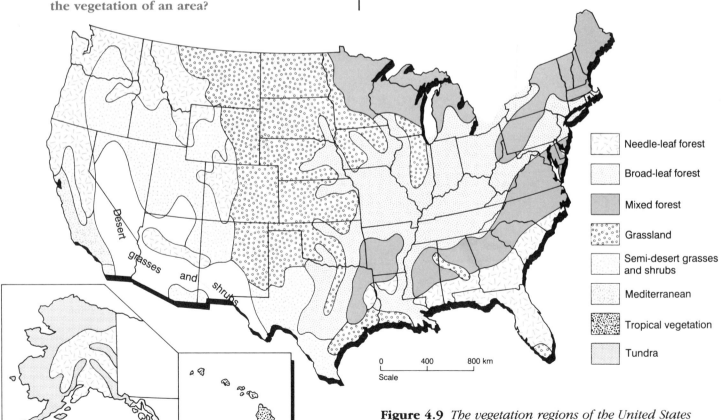

Needle-leaf forest

Broad-leaf forest

Mixed forest

Grassland

Semi-desert grasses and shrubs

Mediterranean

Tropical vegetation

Tundra

**Figure 4.9** *The vegetation regions of the United States*

| REGION | AVERAGE TEMPERATURES | | PRECIPITATION | VEGETATION |
| --- | --- | --- | --- | --- |
| | JANUARY | JULY | | |
| The Appalachian Mountains | | | | |
| The Gulf-Atlantic Coastal Lowlands and Piedmont | | | | |
| The Interior and Great Plains | | | | |
| The Interior Highlands | | | | |
| The Rocky Mountains | | | | |
| The Intermontane Basins and Plateaus | | | | |
| The Pacific Ranges and Coastal Lowlands | | | | |
| The Canadian Shield | | | | |
| Arctic Coastal Plain | | | | |
| The Volcanic Islands of Hawaii | | | | |

*SAMPLE ONLY*

# Understanding Concepts

2. Select an appropriate answer for each of the spaces in the table from the list in the shaded box. Complete the table in your notebook.

| REGION | NATURAL RESOURCE | PRIMARY INDUSTRIES |
| --- | --- | --- |
| The Appalachian Mountains | | |
| The Gulf-Atlantic Coastal Lowlands and Piedmont | | |
| The Interior and Great Plains | | |
| The Interior Highlands | | |
| The Rocky Mountains | | |
| The Intermontane Basins and Plateaus | | |
| The Pacific Ranges and Coastal Lowlands | | |
| The Canadian Shield | | |
| Arctic Coastal Plain | | |
| The Volcanic Islands of Hawaii | | |

*SAMPLE ONLY*

**Pool of Words** (these may be used more than once)
Oil and natural gas, forest, mining, lumber, farming, agriculture, cotton, flat land, rich soils, iron ore, unusual landforms, irrigated farming, fishing

# Enrichment

3. The lines on Figure 4.6 joining places with the same average January temperatures are known as **isotherms**. What do you think the isotherms would look like if only distance from the equator influenced the January temperature? What would they look like if only distance from the ocean had an influence? What would they look like if only altitude affected the temperature?

4. Write a paragraph to explain the relationship among these factors:
   (a) landscape features    (c) precipitation
   (b) temperature          (d) vegetation.

5. In which of the ten landscape regions would you prefer to live? Why?

# CHAPTER 5

# Geography, People, and Industry

**C**hapter 4 described the physical geography of the United States. It showed how the physical geography influences the distribution of primary industries such as forestry, mining, and farming. This chapter examines the human geography of the country, including **settlement patterns, population growth**, the **distribution of population**, and **migration patterns**. All these aspects of human geography influence the distribution of employment in the **secondary** and **tertiary** sectors of the economy.

## FOCUS QUESTIONS

1. **What influence does the geography of the United States have on the location and distribution of secondary and tertiary industries?**

2. **How do settlement patterns affect the distribution of industry?**

## CONCEPTS

| | |
|---|---|
| settlement patterns | transportation |
| expansion | secondary industry |
| manifest destiny | tertiary industry |

# Settlement and Growth of the United States

Figure 5.1 shows the expansion of the United States since the American War of Independence (1776–1783). Land was gained through purchase, treaties, and wars.

England **ceded** or gave up much of the land west of the original Thirteen Colonies in 1783. This land included most of the area east of the Mississippi River. Other ceded land came from Spain and Mexico. Surprisingly, a great deal of land was simply purchased from various European powers. In 1803, the French government sold the land west of the Mississippi to the Americans for only $15 million in what became known as the Louisiana Purchase. **Napoleon Bonaparte** sold the land because he needed money to finance his wars in Europe. Alaska was purchased from Russia in 1867 for $7.2 million. The Russian czar needed money to pay for the Crimean War, so he convinced the reluctant Americans to buy Alaska. The sale was so unpopular that it passed in the United States Congress by only one vote! Critics called it "Seward's Icebox" and "Seward's Folly" after Secretary of State **William Seward**, who negotiated the deal with Russia.

The United States also gained land through **annexations** and wars. Texas won independence from Mexico in 1836 after a brief war. It was annexed by the United States in 1845. That same year, President **James Polk** offered to buy California and New Mexico from Mexico for $30 million; however, the Mexicans did not want

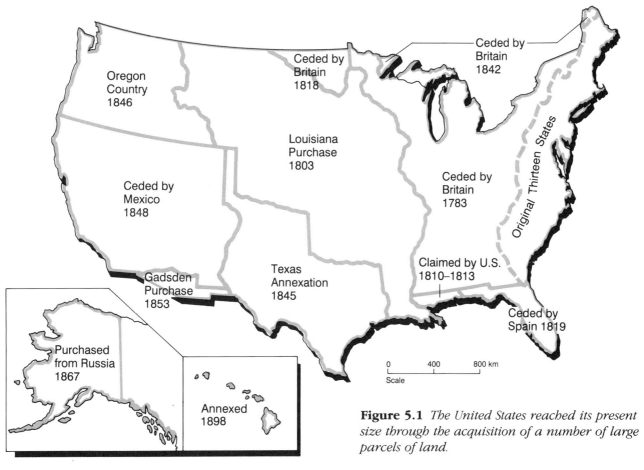

**Figure 5.1** *The United States reached its present size through the acquisition of a number of large parcels of land.*

to sell and went to war over the issue. After a series of military defeats, Mexico signed the Treaty of Guadalupe–Hidalgo in 1848, selling the United States California and New Mexico for only $13 million. In addition, Texas was extended south to the Rio Grande. With the 49th parallel fixed as the northern border between Canada and the United States in 1846, the continental U.S. was complete.

The newly acquired lands did not immediately become states. Statehood came over a number of years, with the federal government controlling the sparsely settled lands. This is the pattern that occurred in many federations, including Canada and Australia. In fact, both Canada and Australia still have large areas, known as territories, that are administered directly by their federal governments, rather than by provincial or state governments. In the United States, the last four states to be admitted to the Union were New Mexico (1912), Arizona (1912), Alaska (1959), and Hawaii (1959). There are now 50 states in the Union.

### PROGRESS CHECK

1. **Estimate the percentage of land gained by the United States through purchases and through cessions.**
2. **Why were European countries willing to sell large areas of land to the United States?**
3. **How were California and New Mexico acquired by the United States? Why do you suppose the U.S. wanted to control these parts of the continent?**

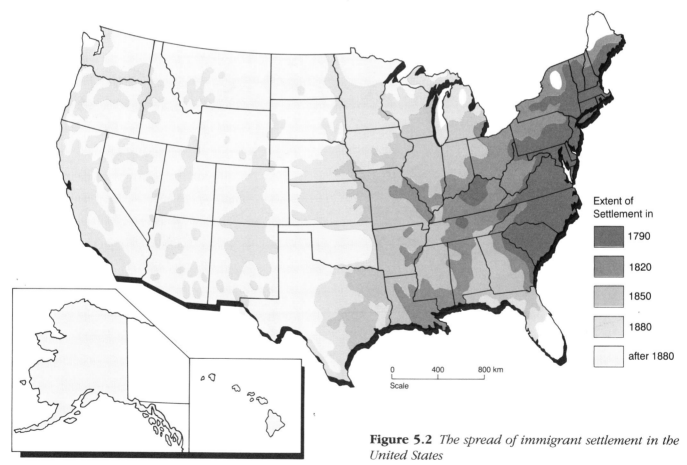

**Figure 5.2** *The spread of immigrant settlement in the United States*

Extent of Settlement in

1790
1820
1850
1880
after 1880

0   400   800 km
Scale

## Westward Settlement

The spread of settlement in the United States was from east to west as shown in Figure 5.2. The original Thirteen Colonies were settled by people coming from Britain and the countries of continental Europe. The first settlements were built at places with convenient access to the mother countries. These settlements, spread along the Atlantic Coast, grew to become some of the oldest cities in North America. Settlement moved west as new land became part of the United States. Variations on this pattern occurred when parts of the West Coast were settled by "forty-niners" during the California gold rush of 1849. The dry interior lands were only settled after 1880.

The westward movement to occupy and control much of the North American continent was seen by many Americans as their country's **manifest destiny**. Manifest destiny was a slogan coined in 1845 by **John O'Sullivan**, editor of the *New York Morning News*, who wrote this passage in support of the annexation of Texas:

> . . . our manifest destiny [is] to overspread and to possess the whole of the continent which Providence has given us for the development of the great experiment of liberty and federated self-government entrusted to us.

This idea that the United States should rule the North American continent was a matter of concern to Mexico in the South and Canada in the North.

**Figure 5.3** *A famous painting of "Manifest Destiny" by **John Gast** shows the goddess of Destiny guiding American expansion with a book in one hand and a telegraph line in the other.*

The westward expansion of the United States was directly encouraged by the passing of the Homestead Act in 1862. This Act gave thousands of immigrants free land on the Great Plains. Quarter sections of land were available on condition that farmers build a house and farm the land within a given period of time.

The Homestead Act is an example of how the government encouraged economic development in the West. They also helped private businesses build railroads. Once the rail lines were built, the railroads were able to earn a profit transporting people to the West and shipping agricultural products and minerals back to the industrialized East. Other private companies benefited from the railroad building and expansion in trade. In the end, the government gained control of the new land and acquired an expanding tax base. Government, business, and labour all benefited.

There was a dark side to this expansion. The land opened for settlement really was not empty for it was occupied by many different native peoples. They were the innocent victims of this

expansion and development. Their nomadic, pre-industrial lifestyle clashed with the European settlers. One tribe after another was forced to give up traditional life as settlers claimed ownership of the open land. The Indians of the Plains, for example, relied upon the buffalo for

**Figure 5.5** *As a result of the settlement of the West, the native peoples were confined to reservations. Their traditional lifestyles were destroyed.*

**Figure 5.4** *A sod house in Nebraska in the late 1800s. Why was sod used as a building material?*

their existence. In 1865, it was estimated that there were 15 million buffalo roaming free west of the Mississippi River. By 1885, there were only 25 animals left! The very lifeblood of the Indians was destroyed in one generation. This is only one of many examples of the drastic impact of white settlers on the lives of native peoples. Initially, most were forced to live on reservations and accept government welfare in order to survive.

## PROGRESS CHECK

1. **Why are the oldest settlements in North America on the East Coast?**
2. **What is meant by the term "manifest destiny"?**
3. **What was the impact of the settlement of the West on the life of the native peoples?**

## Growth of the Transportation System

Expansion of the population and settlement of the West resulted in a need for a fast, efficient, and economical means of transportation and communication across the whole country. In 1857, Wells, Fargo and Company organized a stagecoach service from St. Louis to San Francisco. In the early 1860s, they added the Pony Express service. Using 150 stations stocked with fresh horses, the Pony Express guaranteed delivery of a letter from Missouri to California within ten days. But after only 18 months of operation, this service was made obsolete by a new technology called the **telegraph**. The telegraph could transmit a message in seconds, not days.

**Figure 5.6** *The Pony Express was replaced by a new technology — the telegraph.*

Meanwhile, as early as 1849, the United States Senate had considered the building of a railroad to the West Coast. The Pacific Railroad Act, passed in 1862, authorized a route from Omaha, Nebraska, to San Francisco, California. The final spike, a golden one for ceremonial purposes, was driven in at Promontory Point in Utah in 1869. Figure 5.7 shows this first railway line and other early transcontinental railways.

These early routes across the continent included the Northern Pacific from Lake Superior to Tacoma, Washington, and the Southern Pacific from San Francisco through Los Angeles to New Orleans. Figure 5.7 shows the substantial land grants that the companies were given by the United States government to finance the construction of these lines. The companies

received a 120 km right of way. This meant that they owned 60 km of land on either side of the rail line. With the coming of the railway, the value of this land increased because it was close to the railway line.

Railroad construction reached its peak of nearly 420 000 km of track by 1920. At that point, automobiles began to take over as the major means of transport. There were about 8000 automobiles in the United States in 1900, but that number rose to eight million passenger cars and one million trucks by 1920. The increase in the importance of the automobile was dependent on the growth of a network of roads. In 1904, practically all rural roads were little better than dirt tracks. By 1924, there were over 750 000 km of rural highways with paved surfaces. New

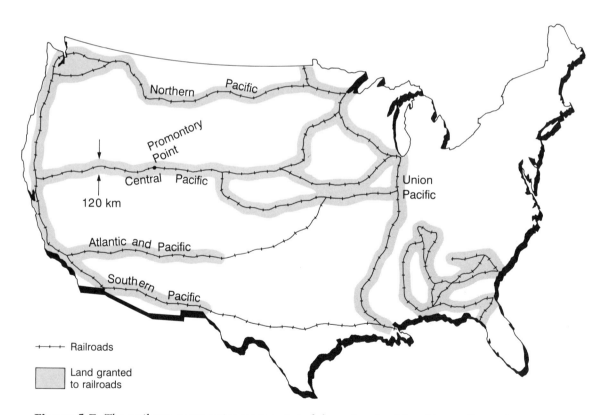

**Figure 5.7** *The railway companies were granted huge tracts of land to motivate them to construct lines in the American West. Why did the government want to encourage the development of the West?*

highways were being added to at a rate of 60 000 km a year, at an annual cost of over $1 billion. In the 1920s, the automobile rivaled the train as a means of passenger transportation; within a few more years, it would become more popular for both short- and long-distance journeys. Trains have continued to be important for long-distance freight transportation to the present time, especially for bulk raw materials like coal, iron ore, or grain.

As with the railroads, the American government helped finance the development of the highway system. The Federal Aid Highway Act was passed by Congress in 1956. This Act provided for the construction of the Interstate Highway System, a new road network of almost 70 000 km. When it is finished, it will connect more than 90 percent of the cities in the country with populations greater than 50 000. The provision of an efficient transportation network is one of the important functions of government. This kind of service, paid for by tax dollars, stimulates the growth of the economy.

## Recent Changes in the Transportation System

There have been many changes in transportation patterns since the end of World War II in 1945. At that time, commercial airlines only carried about three million passengers a year. Airports were small and commercial aircraft were able to carry only 20 to 40 passengers. In the late 1960s, wide-bodied jets like the Boeing 747, which can carry about 500 passengers, were introduced. By this time, there were over 60 million passengers annually and aircraft were becoming important as freight carriers. Since then, aircraft travel has become so popular that Chicago's O'Hare Airport (the busiest in the United States) alone handles about 60 million passengers a year on almost 800 000 flights. At peak periods, this airport has up to 210 takeoffs and landings an hour.

The railroads have not shared in the post-war growth experienced by airlines, automobiles, and trucks. For most of this century, rail traffic has declined, to the point where companies are not making profits. In 1970, the United States government established the Amtrak system to run the country's intercity passenger trains. This allowed the private railroad companies to concentrate on the movement of freight. Even so, many railroad companies continue to lose money.

## PROGRESS CHECK

1. **What advantages did the telegraph have over the Pony Express?**
2. **In 1865, there were 56 000 km of railroad track in the United States. In 1900, there was five times as many kilometres. What reasons can you suggest to explain such a rapid rate of growth?**
3. **What form of transportation replaced the train for moving passengers? What form of transportation is used by most passengers today?**

## Recent Population and Migration Patterns

The present distribution of population still reflects historical settlement patterns. Those areas that were settled early have remained among the most densely populated regions, while those areas settled more recently are more lightly populated.

During the past 30 years, there has been a movement from the northern states, which have been referred to as the Frost Belt, to the more southerly parts of the country, the Sun Belt.

Many of the Sun Belt states have important new industries, such as tourism and recreation. Other high-growth states have glamorous, "high-tech" industries. These states include Texas and California. A few states like Alaska and Wyoming have grown because of their natural resources —

oil in the case of Alaska and coal in Wyoming. The states which have experienced the least growth in recent years are mainly in the North and Northeast. These are states whose economies are based on traditional **"smokestack" industries**, such as iron and steel making. In recent years, offshore competition and aging factories have caused these industries to experience some difficult times.

**Figure 5.8**  *The population distribution of the United States. In the Northeast, a number of towns and cities have grown together to form a huge, urbanized region called a **megalopolis**. The "Boswash" megalopolis stretches from Boston in the North to Washington in the South.*

# Factors Affecting Industrial Locations

There are three basic types of industries — primary, secondary, and tertiary. Primary industries were described in Chapter 4. They are sometimes called resource industries because they extract the natural resources found in our environment. Examples of these industries include mining, fishing, forestry, and farming.

**Secondary industries** further process the raw materials supplied by primary industries. Growing cotton is a primary industry, but the manufacture of garments from the cotton is a secondary industry. Other examples of secondary

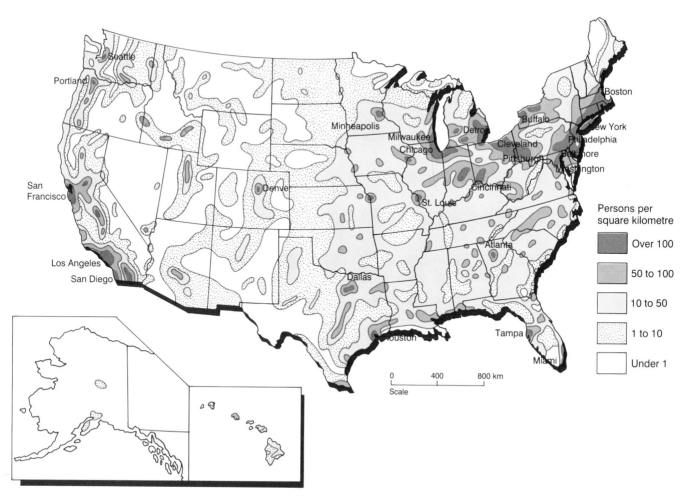

Persons per
square kilometre

Over 100

50 to 100

10 to 50

1 to 10

Under 1

0    400    800 km

Scale

**60**

industries include the construction, automobile, and steel industries. These activities can be divided into two different groups based on the characteristics of their finished products. **Durable goods** are such things as kitchen appliances, electronic equipment, and automobiles. This category also includes machinery and equipment used in factories. **Non-durable goods** are those that are consumed, such as food and clothing.

**Tertiary industries** provide services. There are many types of tertiary industries, generally grouped into the categories of transportation, public utilities, wholesale and retail trade, finance, insurance, and real estate. People who work as barbers, cooks, mechanics, lawyers, doctors, and teachers are employed in the tertiary sector of the economy. Table 5.1 shows how employment in primary, secondary, and tertiary industries changed from 1941 to 1987.

**Table 5.1** *Employment in the United States*

| EMPLOYMENT SECTORS | NUMBERS ROUNDED TO THE NEAREST MILLION | |
|---|---|---|
| | 1941 | 1987 |
| Total Number Employed All Sectors | 50 | 112 |
| PRIMARY SECTOR: | | |
| Agriculture and Mining | 10 | 4 |
| SECONDARY SECTOR: | | |
| Construction and Manufacturing | 15 | 24 |
| TERTIARY SECTOR: | | |
| Transportation and Public Utilities | 3 | 5 |
| Trade, Wholesale and Retail | 7 | 24 |
| Finance, Insurance and Real Estate | 2 | 7 |
| Personal Services | 4 | 24 |
| Federal, State and Local Government | 6 | 17 |

## Locating Secondary Industries

In the real world, there are many factors influencing the location of secondary industries. Here are some of the more important considerations.

### THE MARKET FACTOR

For some industries, a location within their market is extremely important. This is necessary to reduce transportation costs and to provide after-sales service. Perishable products are manufactured close to their markets to avoid spoiling.

### THE COST AND SKILLS OF LABOUR

Both the cost and quality of labour are important in determining the location of some industries. One reason that has been cited for the recent growth of manufacturing industry in the Sun Belt is the fact that there is less unionized labour, making wage rates lower. Wages for workers are usually a significant cost of any manufacturing industry, and today, are more important than transportation costs in many industries. This is especially true of those industries producing electrical and electronic goods.

### RAW MATERIALS

Often a major factor in locating a manufacturing industry is the raw materials. Some industries use large amounts of raw materials in their processing, part of which is consumed in the production process or ends up as waste. A good example would be the iron and steel industry. The finished product may be only one-quarter of the weight of the raw materials, so the processing plants are usually located near the raw materials. In other cases, transporting the raw materials is easier or less expensive than moving the finished goods. These industries tend to locate near their markets.

## FUEL AND POWER

During the Industrial Revolution, water power from rivers and coal from coal fields were important in determining the location of industry. Today, power sources do not generally attract manufacturing industry because power can be transported cheaply over great distances in the form of electricity.

## SITE AND SERVICES

Large amounts of flat land may be needed for some large-scale industries—car manufacturing, oil refining, aircraft production, the manufacturing of recreational vehicles, and the like. Governments frequently try to attract industries by providing serviced land in **industrial parks** that are designed to help industries avoid problems in setting up new facilities.

## CLIMATE

In the past, climate was important to the location of manufacturing industries. The damp climates of Lancashire and the New England states helped the textile industries by making the fibres easier to work with. Today, climate can be artificially controlled and is therefore less important in determining the location of industry. There are some exceptions, though. The film industry is still tied to Hollywood partly because of the warm, sunny climate.

## GOVERNMENT INTERVENTION

Federal, state, and municipal governments often try to attract manufacturing industry by offering special incentives. Figure 5.9 shows an advertisement paid for by the government of the state of Vermont to attract companies.

## GEOGRAPHICAL INERTIA

Sometimes a manufacturing plant will be in what seems to be a poor location. This may be because it located there a long time ago when the site was a good place to build the plant. It might now be too costly to move to a location better suited to present-day conditions. This tendency for industries to remain in their existing locations rather than move is known as **geographical inertia**.

**Figure 5.9** *A state-sponsored advertisement to attract manufacturing industry to Maine*

## PROGRESS CHECK

1. Define these terms:
   (a) primary industry
   (b) secondary industry
   (c) tertiary industry.
2. In one or two sentences, explain how each of these factors influences decisions to locate secondary industries:
   (a) location of the market
   (b) sources of raw materials
   (c) government initiatives.
3. For each of these manufacturing activities, decide what would be the three most important factors to consider when choosing a new location:
   (a) a cookie factory
   (b) an airplane manufacturing plant
   (c) a paper mill.
   Give reasons to explain your answers.

## A Simplified Model for Locating an Iron Ore Processing Plant: The Varignon Frame

Imagine that you need to find the best location for an iron ore processing plant. The industry requires coal, limestone, and iron ore as its main raw materials. (Assume that limestone is found everywhere, so you do not need to be concerned about it.) The amount of iron ore needed to produce 1 t of iron will depend upon the quality of the iron ore. Some iron ore, known as haematite and magnetite, is 70 percent pure while taconite is only 30 percent pure. The less pure the ore, the more you need to make 1 t of iron. For this example, assume that the ore is about 33 percent pure, which means that 3 t of ore are needed to produce 1 t of pig iron.

Coal is used as a **reducing agent** to help remove oxygen from the iron ore. One tonne of coal is needed to produce 1 t of pig iron. Using 3 t of iron ore and 1 t of coal to produce 1 t of

pig iron means that the finished product is about one-quarter of the weight of the raw materials (again, ignoring the limestone). The Varignon frame can now be used to help find a location for the processing plant that minimizes transportation costs. The Varignon frame is shown in Figure 5.10.

The frame is a triangle with the points of the triangle (the vertices) representing the locations of the coal deposit, the iron ore deposit, and the market. To determine the best location for the plant, three pieces of string are passed through a ring at each vertex of the triangle (as shown in the diagram) and attached to a central ring. At the other ends of the strings are weights representing the weight of iron ore, the weight of coal, and the weight of the pig iron produced. If the weight of iron ore was set at 300 g, the weight of coal would be 100 g and the weight of pig iron 100 g.

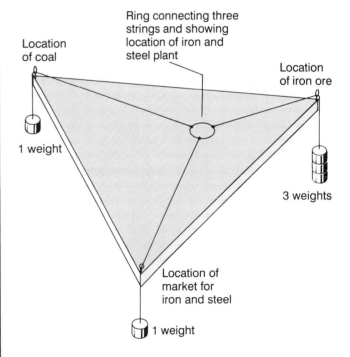

**Figure 5.10** *The Varignon frame*

The heavy weight of the iron ore tends to pull the central ring toward it; however, the weights for coal and market location are also pulling the ring. The place where the central ring ends up is the best location for the iron ore processing plant. At this point, transportation costs would be reduced to their lowest possible value, assuming transportation costs for each commodity are equal.

## The Location of Service Industries

The rate of growth for service industries is much faster than for primary or secondary industries. Locating a service industry is not as complex as locating a manufacturing industry. Generally, service industries locate where people live. Every city needs plumbers, teachers, entertainers, lawyers, and so on. As cities grow, more service industries are needed. Some specialized services are located in the largest population centres and, of course, federal and state government services are concentrated in the federal and state capital cities.

# Summary

Human geography is a term used to refer to the patterns of human activity on the surface of the earth. In this chapter, you have examined settlement patterns, population growth and distribution, and migration patterns. These patterns are in part caused by the physical geography of the country. Together, the physical and human geographies have shaped the industrial activities of the United States.

# Checking Back

1. From your understanding of primary, secondary, and tertiary industries, list five examples of jobs in each industry.
2. Match the terms in the two columns to identify how the different states were acquired by the United States.

| STATE | METHOD |
|---|---|
| Alaska | ceded |
| California | purchased |
| Texas | war |
| Oregon | annexed |

3. Use examples from the chapter to show how new technologies developed between 1800 and the 1980s changed the way people travelled.
4. Figure 5.11 shows the distribution of manufacturing industries across the United States. Pick three types of industry and, using information from this chapter, explain why they are concentrated where they are.

# Understanding Concepts

5. In a sentence or two, suggest how each of the following people would probably have felt about the settlement of the West following passage of the Homestead Act of 1862:

   (a) politician
   (b) settler
   (c) an entrepreneur
   (d) a native Indian.

6. Select one of the following modes of transportation and briefly describe the growth and importance of the industry over time, until the present:

   (a) railroads
   (b) automobiles and trucks
   (c) airplanes.

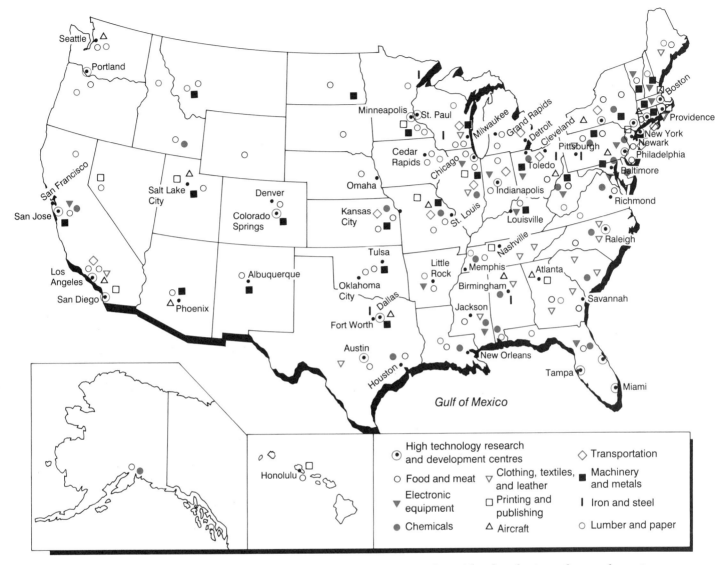

**Figure 5.11** *The distribution of manufacturing activity across the United States*

# Enrichment

7. Will electronic mail do to the postal service what the telegraph did to the Pony Express? Explain your opinion.

8. Research the ways in which the opening of the American and Canadian Wests were the same, and the ways in which they were different.

9. Why did Mexico lose the war with the United States in 1846? Research the key battles to find an answer to this question.

10. Prepare a report on the impact of American settlers on the native Indians.

# CHAPTER 6

# Government, Business, and Labour

This chapter is about the role of government, business, and labour in the American economy. These three groups often have different, and sometimes conflicting, interests. The people who run businesses want to make the maximum profit and workers want the highest wages possible. These two groups must settle their differences and work together because they need each other. The government acts as a kind of referee, setting rules and regulations to help smooth relationships.

## FOCUS QUESTIONS

1. **What roles do government, business, and labour play in the American market economy?**
2. **How do the three groups interact with each other?**

## CONCEPTS

| | |
|---|---|
| **institutions** | **role of business** |
| **role of government** | **role of labour** |
| **corporations** | **labour organizations** |

# Government, Business, and Labour Institutions

Government, business, and labour have developed a number of **institutions**, organizations that have specific purposes. An example of a government institution is the Congress. A bank is an example of a business institution, while the AFL-CIO union is an example of a labour institution. All institutions have a structure or **organization**, a stated **purpose**, **support** from some segment of the population, and some degree of **power**.

Usually, institutions are organized in the form of **hierarchies**, within which people have particular roles to play. The people at the top, presidents and chairpersons, have the greatest power and influence while those farther down the hierarchy have less power. To get more influence, people "move up the ladder." The incentive for promotion in a market economy usually is greater pay and prestige.

Each institution has a purpose. The purpose of a business corporation in a market economy is to make a profit for shareholders. This is not necessarily the case for a publicly owned business, such as the post office. Its goal might be to provide an efficient and fair service to all citizens. To meet this goal, the government might keep postal rates low and subsidize the post office with tax dollars. It is important to identify the purpose of an institution because it can vary widely.

Institutions must have the **approval** of the population they serve. If the postal service is inadequate, the government will feel pressure from citizens to make changes. Privately owned businesses must satisfy their customers and their shareholders or they will go out of business. This need for approval is a powerful force in a market economy. You will see in Chapter 8 how ordinary consumers can force huge corporations to make changes.

There are many restraints on the power of any institution. This is particularly true in a free market economy where voters and consumers have the ultimate power. Voters decide who gets elected and consumers decide which businesses will be successful when they purchase their products or services.

As you study each of the institutions in this chapter, use a chart to gather and organize information. The chart could look like the one below.

| INSTITUTION | ORGANIZATION | PURPOSE | APPROVAL | POWER |
|---|---|---|---|---|
| Government | | | | |
| Business | | SAMPLE ONLY | | |

Complete the chart using brief points.

# The Role of Government in the American Economy

Governments have two basic roles. The first role has to do with the regulation of economic activity. While all governments have some role in their economies, this role is very different in each country. The American market economy has the least amount of government regulation. The amount of government control increases in a mixed economy and is even greater in a socialist economy. Finally, a centrally planned economy is almost completely controlled by the government. (See Fig. 6.1)

The second role of government is to provide services for the people, everything from mail delivery to military defence and social programs. Since demand for government funds is always greater than the funds available, decisions have to be made on spending. These choices are expressed in the federal budget, a statement of how tax dollars and other revenues will be spent.

**67**

**Figure 6.1** *The amount of government control of the economy varies in each country.*

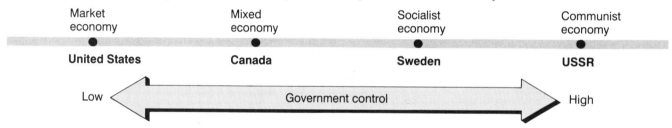

| Market economy | Mixed economy | Socialist economy | Communist economy |
|---|---|---|---|
| **United States** | **Canada** | **Sweden** | **USSR** |

Low ← Government control → High

The government of the United States is based upon the Constitution developed in 1787 and first ratified by the state of Delaware in December of that year. It was signed on September 17, 1787, by 39 delegates at a conference in Philadelphia. The Constitution established the main government institutions.

The Constitution divides power among three separate branches of government—legislative, executive, and judicial.

The president and an appointed staff of advisors make up the **executive branch** of the American federal government. The president proposes and vetoes legislation, appoints judges, and acts as the supreme commander of the military forces. The executive branch has other powers that are shown in Figure 6.3.

**Figure 6.2** *The Constitution of the United States is a "living" document. To reflect the changing needs of the people, the Constitution has been amended 26 times since 1787.*

The **judicial branch** is made up of the Supreme Court and other federal courts. It is an independent part of the government and can overturn a law if it is unconstitutional. In other words, no one is above the law. Everyone, even the president, the military, and Congress, is bound by the Constitution.

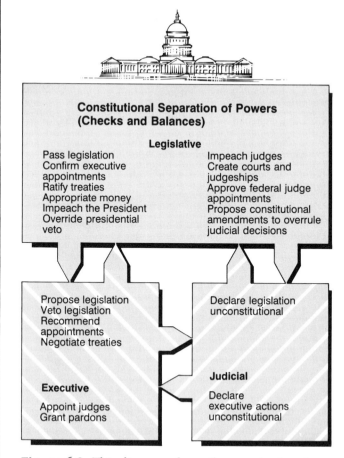

**Constitutional Separation of Powers (Checks and Balances)**

**Legislative**

| | |
|---|---|
| Pass legislation | Impeach judges |
| Confirm executive appointments | Create courts and judgeships |
| Ratify treaties | Approve federal judge appointments |
| Appropriate money | Propose constitutional amendments to overrule judicial decisions |
| Impeach the President | |
| Override presidential veto | |

Propose legislation
Veto legislation
Recommend appointments
Negotiate treaties

Declare legislation unconstitutional

**Executive**

Appoint judges
Grant pardons

**Judicial**

Declare executive actions unconstitutional

**Figure 6.3** *This diagram shows the constitutional separation of powers in the United States government.*

The **legislative branch** of the government consists of the Senate and the House of Representatives. The Senate has 100 members, two from every state, while the House of Representatives has 435 members (1989). The number of representatives is based on population. California, as the largest state, has the most members (45), while the states of Alaska, Delaware, North Dakota, South Dakota, Vermont, and Wyoming have only one each. This is one reason why the population distribution discussed in the last chapter is so important. Population size has a direct impact on political power.

Another level of government in the United States is state government. The states also regulate economic activities and provide services. Figure 6.4 shows the powers given to the federal and state governments under the Constitution. As well, it lists those powers which are denied to them.

**Figure 6.4** *The powers of federal and state governments in the United States*

| Federal Government | Federal and State Governments | State Governments |
|---|---|---|
| **Enumerated powers delegated to the Congress:**<br><br>• to regulate interstate and foreign commerce<br>• to establish laws governing citizenship<br>• to coin money<br>• to control the postal system<br>• to regulate patents and copyrights<br>• to establish federal courts lower than the Supreme Court<br>• to declare war<br>• to establish and support the armed forces<br>• to pass all laws necessary and proper for carrying out the preceding powers | **Concurrent powers shared by the federal and state governments:**<br><br>• to tax<br>• to borrow money<br>• to establish penal laws<br>• to charter banks<br>• to take property for public purposes by eminent domain | **Reserved powers retained by the state governments:**<br><br>• to regulate suffrage for state elections<br>• to maintain a system of public education<br>• to establish marriage and divorce laws<br>• to establish laws governing corporations<br>• to establish traffic laws<br>• to regulate intrastate commerce<br>• Amendment 10 of the Constitution reserves to the state governments all powers not delegated to the federal government or prohibited by the Constitution. |

**Prohibited Powers**

| Powers denied the federal government: | Powers denied the federal and state governments: | Powers denied the state governments: |
|---|---|---|
| • to suspend the writ of *habeas corpus* except in cases of rebellion or invasion<br>• to levy taxes on exports<br>• to give preferential treatment in commerce or revenue to the ports of any state<br>• to draw money from the Treasury except by appropriation under a specific law<br>• to permit persons holding federal office to accept gifts from a foreign country without consent of Congress | • to pass bills of attainder<br>• to pass *ex post facto* laws<br>• to grant titles of nobility | • to enter into treaties with other nations or with other states without the consent of Congress<br>• to coin money<br>• to impair obligations of contract<br>• to place a tax on imports or exports except to carry out their inspection laws<br>• to keep troops or ships in time of peace without consent of Congress |

Both governments have many powers which influence other institutions. For example, they can give charters for banks. The federal government regulates interstate and foreign commerce while the state governments establish laws governing business corporations. Both levels of government can levy taxes. The federal government regulates the patent system.

**Municipal governments** provide services for the local population, such as city planning and zoning regulations, fire and police protection, recreation facilities, public health and sanitation services, street maintenance, waste disposal, and water services. Their main sources of revenue are property and business taxes.

## How the Government Affects the Economy

The Federal Reserve System controls the supply of money. Because of this, it has a great impact on the economy. The government can increase economic activity by increasing the supply of money. Such action usually causes loan interest rates to fall which means that individual consumers and businesses can borrow at a lower cost. This stimulates people to spend more; however, too much spending can lead to **inflation**. Inflation occurs when there is an increase in the cost of living as a result of increasing prices. In simple terms, increased demand has driven prices up, so people have to pay more. When this happens, the government can reduce the supply of money to push up interest rates and slow down spending. This kind of government intervention plays an important role in the American market economy.

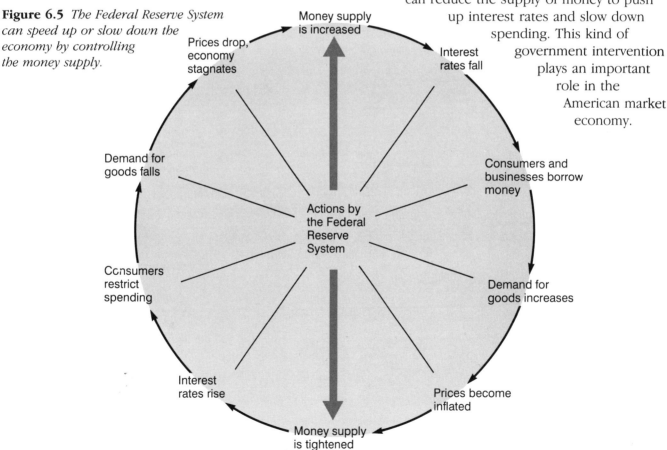

**Figure 6.5** *The Federal Reserve System can speed up or slow down the economy by controlling the money supply.*

Money supply is increased

Interest rates fall

Prices drop, economy stagnates

Consumers and businesses borrow money

Demand for goods falls

Actions by the Federal Reserve System

Consumers restrict spending

Demand for goods increases

Interest rates rise

Prices become inflated

Money supply is tightened

## The Department of Justice: A Government Institution

The Department of Justice is one part of the executive branch of the federal government. This department investigates and prosecutes all violations of federal law. It is headed by the attorney-general who is appointed by the president, with the approval of the Senate. Among the more important activities that the Department of Justice handles are:

- the enforcement of antitrust laws;
- civil suits and claims involving the federal government;
- federal criminal cases;
- lawsuits relating to national lands, pollution, and property;
- lawsuits based on federal tax laws; and
- lawsuits dealing with civil rights.

This institution affects the market economy in many ways. For example, antitrust laws are used to break up business monopolies, and corporations are sued for violating pollution laws. This department also ensures that tax laws are enforced and that individuals and businesses pay their taxes. On the other hand, the government can be taken to court by an individual or business if too much tax is taken. In theory, all groups and individuals have equal access to the law: no individual or group is above the law. This is an important principle in the American market economy.

### PROGRESS CHECK

1. **Briefly describe the four characteristics of an institution.**
2. **What are the two basic roles of government?**
3. **What is meant by inflation?**
4. **Prepare a chart summarizing the organization, purpose, approval, and power of the Department of Justice.**

# Business Corporations

Shortly after his election in 1924, President **Calvin Coolidge** stated that "the chief business of the American people is business. They are profoundly concerned with producing, selling, investing, and prospering in the world." Later, he praised American business as "one of the great contributing forces to the moral and spiritual advancement of the human race." While Coolidge may have been overstating the case, there is no doubt that business has a fundamental importance in the everyday lives of Americans. One of the most important forms of business is the **corporation**.

A corporation is an organization that can own property and make **contracts** just as though it were an individual person. Corporations are usually owned by a number of people who hold **shares**. They are subject to a whole range of federal, state, and local laws and regulations; however, they have several advantages over other types of business. First, they can raise huge amounts of money through the public sale of stock or shares in the company. Second, the shareholders have a **limited liability**. If the corporation goes bankrupt, they will lose only the money that they invested in the form of shares, and not their other assets, such as their houses, cars, or savings. The third advantage is that large corporations with many shareholders have the stability of group ownership. There are about three million corporations in the United States.

The corporation is just one of four types of business ownership that are common in the United States. The other types include **single proprietorships** (of which there are about 13 million) and **partnerships** (about 1.5 million). Single proprietorships are small stores and businesses owned by one person. Partnerships are common in medicine, law, real estate, and retailing. They are an agreement between two or more people who own a business. A single proprietorship or even a partnership may go out of business if the owner or one of the partners dies or decides to quit. The fourth type of business, the **franchise**, has become very popular in the last few decades and will be discussed separately in Chapter 8.

## Corporate Organization

The organization of a corporation is shown in Figure 6.6. The shareholders are the owners of the corporation. The number of shareholders may vary from a few family members to millions of individuals and investment companies. Table 6.1 shows some of the American companies with the largest number of shareholders at the end of 1987.

Shareholders elect a board of directors to set policies and goals for their company. The board of directors hires senior officers who handle the day-to-day operations of the company. Shareholders vote on important matters of concern to the company, usually at the annual meeting where the company presents its annual report. Corporations are not run like a democracy. Shareholders have one vote for each share they own. Control of a company rests in the hands of any shareholder or group of shareholders that controls more than 50 percent of the shares.

Corporations are an important part of the economic life of the United States because they control much of the wealth of the country. The most common are small corporations, generally with assets of less than $100 000. Large corporations control 70 percent of the United States corporate assets and usually have assets of more than $1 billion. Many industries—banking, insurance, petroleum, and transportation industries, to name some—are dominated by large corporations.

**Figure 6.6** *What influence do small shareholders have on corporations?*

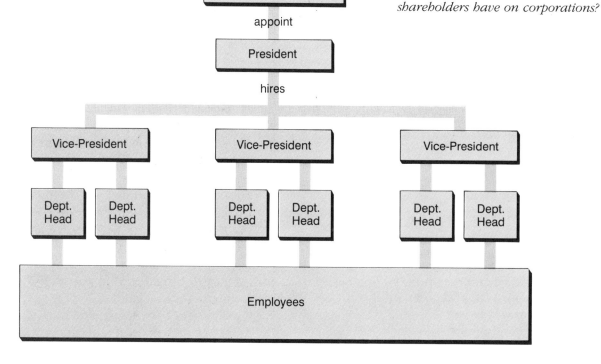

**Table 6.1** *Companies with the Largest Numbers of Shareholders*

| RANK | COMPANY | SHAREHOLDERS |
|------|---------|--------------|
| 1 | American Telephone and Telegraph Co. | 2 782 000 |
| 2 | General Motors | 1 854 000 |
| 3 | BellSouth Corp | 1 578 000 |
| 4 | Bell Atlantic | 1 335 000 |
| 5 | US West | 1 250 000 |
| 10 | International Business Machines (IBM) | 788 000 |
| 11 | Exxon Corp. | 733 000 |
| 12 | General Electric | 506 000 |
| 16 | Sears, Roebuck | 320 000 |
| 20 | Ford Motor | 268 000 |
| 24 | Texaco Inc. | 219 000 |
| 27 | du Pont de Nemours | 209 000 |
| 30 | Chrysler Corp. | 193 000 |
| 38 | Eastman Kodak | 167 000 |

Some corporations have **diversified** by buying other companies. The most common reason for this is that they cannot expand in their established markets. The Reynolds Tobacco Company felt that the market for tobacco products was not growing, so their future in that industry looked bleak. To improve this scenario, they bought various food companies, an oil company, and a transportation company. To project a new image, they changed their name to Reynolds Industries, to let consumers know that they were no longer just a tobacco company. When one company buys a number of other large corporations, it becomes known as a **conglomerate**.

Some corporations have expanded outside of the United States and now own **foreign subsidiaries** in other countries. Many American companies have Canadian subsidiaries with almost the same names, although the word "Canada" is usually added to the names of the subsidiaries. A

recent trend has been for foreign corporations to build subsidiaries in the United States. A Japanese company might build a car manufacturing plant in the United States to avoid the costs of transporting finished cars to North America. This action also avoids **import duties**.

Foreign investment is a mixed blessing. On the positive side is the inflow of foreign capital which creates jobs. On the negative side, it means that control of a part of America's business is in the hands of foreigners, and profits made by the subsidiaries are sent back to the foreign shareholders.

Tables 6.2 and 6.3 list some of the largest business corporations in the United States. The size of a company can be measured either by its **sales** or by its **assets**. Assets include such things as buildings and equipment owned by the company.

**Table 6.2** *The Ten Largest American Businesses*

| FIRM | SALES* | ASSETS* |
|------|--------|---------|
| General Motors | $101 781 000 | $87 421 000 |
| Exxon | $ 76 416 000 | $74 042 000 |
| Ford | $ 71 643 000 | $44 955 000 |
| IBM | $ 54 217 000 | $63 688 000 |
| Mobil | $ 51 223 000 | $41 140 000 |
| General Electric | $ 39 315 000 | $38 920 000 |
| Texaco | $ 34 372 000 | $33 962 000 |
| AT&T | $ 33 598 000 | $38 426 000 |
| du Pont de Nemours | $ 30 468 000 | $28 209 000 |
| Chrysler | $ 26 257 000 | $19 944 000 |

*all figures in thousands

**Table 6.3** *The Five Largest American Retailing Companies*

| FIRM | SALES* | ASSETS* |
|------|--------|---------|
| Sears, Roebuck | $48 439 000 | $74 991 000 |
| K Mart | $25 626 000 | $11 106 000 |
| Safeway Stores | $18 301 000 | $ 4 917 000 |
| Kroger | $17 659 000 | $ 4 397 000 |
| Wal-Mart Stores | $15 959 000 | $ 5 131 000 |

*all figures in thousands

## The Story of a Large American Corporation: Sears, Roebuck and Company

Table 6.3 shows that the largest retailing corporation is the firm of Sears, Roebuck and Company. This company is the largest retailer in the world, with about 830 department stores in the United States and in a number of other countries. Sears also owns several other companies, including the Allstate Insurance Company.

Sears, Roebuck and Company was founded by **Richard Sears** and **Alvah Roebuck** in 1893.

**Figure 6.7**
*Richard Sears*

**Figure 6.8**
*Alvah Roebuck*

Sears began in 1886 selling mail-order watches through newspaper advertising. The next year, he hired Roebuck to repair watches, and in 1893, the two men formed a partnership. By that time, the business had expanded and the firm was selling many products directly from a 322-page catalogue. The partnership was short-lived, however, and in 1895, Roebuck sold his interest in the company to Sears for $25 000. The company continued to prosper and soon became the world's largest mail-order company. Sears died in 1914 a very rich man, but Roebuck ran into financial difficulties, and eventually was forced to go back to the company he had once owned and ask for a job.

Sears, Roebuck and Company opened its first retail store in Chicago in 1925. By 1931, as more stores opened, sales from the retail stores surpassed those from the mail-order catalogue. Today, only about 20 percent of sales comes from the 300 million catalogues that are distributed annually. The firm now has more than 425 000 employees. The headquarters for Sears, Roebuck and Company is still located in Chicago in the Sears Tower. The Sears Tower is a 110-storey building which stands 433 m high, the tallest office building in the world.

## Banks

Banks play a vital role in the American market economy by providing capital in the form of loans for individuals and businesses. There are many different types of banks in the United States, including commercial banks, savings banks, credit unions, and the Federal Reserve System.

The commercial banks are some of the most visible institutions in the United States. These banks have total assets of over $1000 billion, and provide a full range of financial services for businesses and individuals, including chequing and savings accounts, loans, and trust services. While in some countries, there are only a few

74

large commercial banks (in Canada, there are only 11), in the United States, there are many commercial banks, about 15 000 altogether.

**Table 6.4** *The Ten Largest Commercial Banks*

| BANK | ASSETS* | DEPOSITS* |
|------|---------|-----------|
| Citicorp | $203 607 000 | $119 561 000 |
| Chase Manhattan Corp. | $ 99 133 000 | $ 68 578 000 |
| Bankamerica Corp. | $ 92 833 000 | $ 76 290 000 |
| Chemical New York Corp. | $ 78 189 000 | $ 55 509 000 |
| J.P. Morgan & Co. | $ 75 414 000 | $ 43 987 000 |
| Security Pacific Corp. | $ 73 356 000 | $ 45 551 000 |
| Manufacturers Hanover Corp. | $ 73 348 000 | $ 45 176 000 |
| Bankers Trust New York Corp. | $ 56 520 000 | $ 30 220 000 |
| First Interstate Bancorp | $ 50 926 000 | $ 37 569 000 |
| First Chicago Corp. | $ 44 209 000 | $ 31 537 000 |

*all figures in thousands

Like any other business, a bank is run to make money. Individuals and businesses deposit money with the bank, and the bank pays them interest on this money. The bank then lends the money out at a higher interest rate. The difference between what the bank pays to customers and what it charges borrowers is the main source of earnings for the bank. This money is used for the day-to-day operations of the bank, to pay the shareholders' profit, and to pay the salaries of the bank's employees. In addition, the bank has to make up the cost of loans that are not paid back.

The banks must keep some money in reserve to pay customers who have deposited their money and may want to withdraw it at short notice. In the United States, the government has set the percentage which must be kept in reserve at between 3 and 22 percent of the funds deposited. Occasionally, a bank may make too many bad loans that are not repaid. In these situations, the bank itself may go bankrupt and will not be able to pay back the businesses and individuals that have deposited money with it.

The Federal Reserve System was established in 1913. It consists of 12 large regional banks managed by a board of governors. It acts as a bank for the federal government and for the commercial banks around the country, helping them borrow money. Its main role, however, is to control the amount of money in circulation in order to stimulate business, or alternatively, to fight inflation. The Federal Reserve System supervises the ordinary banks to make sure they are being run properly.

**How Banks Make a Profit**

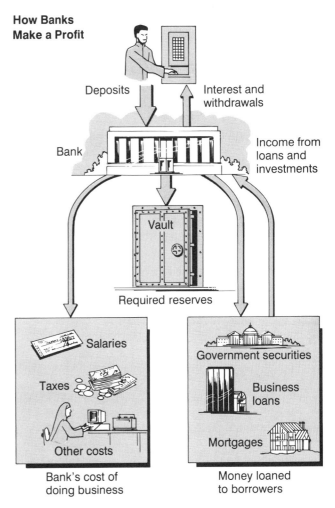

**Figure 6.9** *Banks loan their depositors' money to people who need loans. The interest the banks earn is their source of income.*

## PROGRESS CHECK

1. **What is a corporation? List three advantages that business corporations have over other types of businesses.**
2. **What are some positive and negative effects of foreign ownership?**
3. **What role do banks play in the American economy?**
4. **What is the purpose of the Federal Reserve System?**

# Labour and Labour Organizations

Labour provides the work force for industry. **Labour organizations** help workers gain better wages and working conditions.

The American workplace is changing. Table 6.5 shows the changes from 1830 until 1980. The percentage of people in the work force has grown steadily over the years. This is largely because women have been joining the labour force in increasing numbers since the beginning of the 20th century, and the trend is continuing. In 1981, women represented 43 percent of the civilian labour force in the United States. Six years later, almost 45 percent of the labour force was made up of women. This means that more people are contributing to the nation's labour supply. With both parents working, there is a growing demand for day-care facilities. The provision of day-care is one of the demands that labour organizations now make of employers.

You can see from Table 6.5 that most people worked in farm occupations in the early years of the last century. Today, very few people work on farms, even though farms and agriculture are still important to the economy of the United States. This is because **mechanization** and the use of new technologies have decreased the need for farm workers. In 1820, one farm worker could feed 4.5 people. By 1900, this number rose to eight. In 1960, the number was 26. By 1970, one

farm worker could feed up to 54 people. The impact of new technology in the workplace is a topic both labour organizations and businesses are considering very carefully.

**Table 6.5** *Persons in the Labour Force*

| YEAR | SIZE OF WORK FORCE | PERCENTAGE OF WORKING AGE POPULATION | PERCENTAGE OF LABOUR FORCE IN | |
|------|------|------|------|------|
| | | | FARM WORK | NON-FARM WORK |
| 1830 | 3 932 000 | 45.5 | 70.5 | 29.5 |
| 1900 | 29 073 000 | 50.2 | 37.5 | 62.5 |
| 1950 | 60 054 000 | 53.5 | 11.6 | 88.4 |
| 1980 | 106 085 000 | 62.0 | 2.2 | 97.8 |

Wages in manufacturing industries have risen considerably over the last decades. Average weekly wages rose from $133 in 1970 to $406 in 1987; however, prices have risen at the same rate, so workers are not substantially better off with the higher earnings. Surprisingly, over the same time period, the average manufacturing worker worked 41 hours a week, slightly *more* than in 1970. This goes against a general trend toward shorter work weeks. Wages and hours worked for some non-manufacturing industries are shown in Table 6.6.

**Table 6.6** *Weekly Earnings and Hours Worked in Selected Non-Manufacturing Industries*

| INDUSTRY | 1958 | | 1987 | |
|----------|------|------|------|------|
| | EARNINGS | HOURS | EARNINGS | HOURS |
| Coal mining | $ 98 | 33.3 | $659 | 42.0 |
| Metal mining | $ 95 | 38.6 | $546 | 42.0 |
| Radio/TV | $101 | 38.0 | $394 | 36.3 |
| Transportation | $ 87 | 43.0 | $344 | 38.7 |
| Retail trade | $ 54 | 38.1 | $179 | 29.3 |
| Hotels | $ 41 | 39.7 | $188 | 30.7 |
| Laundries | $ 45 | 38.7 | $210 | 34.2 |

Unions protect and promote the rights and interests of workers. Most workers in the United States, though, are not members of unions. In fact, only about 20 percent of workers belong to unions, although many occupations have associations which perform similar functions. Dentists belong to the American Dental Association, doctors to the American Medical Association, and so on. Even athletes have their own associations. Baseball, hockey, and football all have powerful players associations to negotiate with club owners.

Union membership has been declining in recent decades. The reasons for this are both economic and political. The economy of the United States is changing, and more people now work in tertiary industries where unions are much less influential. Politically, the Republican administration under President **Ronald Reagan** was anti-union. When federal air traffic controllers went on an illegal strike, Reagan simply fired them all rather than negotiate a settlement.

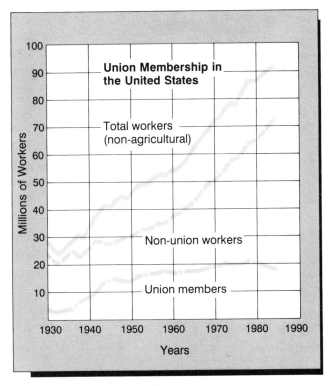

**Figure 6.10** *This graph shows the increase in the size of the American work force since 1930. How successful have unions been in increasing their memberships?*

## The History of Unions and the Rise of the AFL-CIO

Unions began in the early 1800s as a result of abuses by employers against workers. One of the first was the Mechanics Union of Trade Associations, founded in Philadelphia in 1827. Generally, the early unions represented members of a particular trade and were therefore referred to as trade unions. The American Federation of Labour (AFL), founded in 1886, attempted to link the trade unions together into a larger, stronger organization. But even by 1930, unions were still limited to skilled workers, and only 12 percent of workers were members.

A major change in unions occurred in 1935 when **John L. Lewis** formed the Committee for Industrial Organization (CIO). This organization opened its membership to anyone who worked in an industry, not just skilled workers. By 1950, 30 percent of all factory workers were union members. The CIO and AFL were bitterly opposed to each other as they competed for members. It was not until 1955 that the two unions joined together to form the AFL-CIO organization with about 16 million members.

The AFL-CIO is a federation of national unions. About 80 percent of all union members in the United States belong to affiliates of the AFL-CIO organization. The president of the AFL-CIO is the most powerful union leader in the United States, but the AFL-CIO does little in the way of **collective bargaining**. Instead, the organization tries to promote legislation which is favourable to the labour movement. It also tries to improve the public's understanding of unions and to settle conflicts between member unions. In fact, it is trying to increase both the power and the approval of unions, two of the characteristics of institutions mentioned at the beginning of this chapter.

In the 1960s and 1970s, a number of other groups formed unions of a different type. One such union was the United Farm Workers of

America. This union of migrant workers and farm labourers was organized by the charismatic leader, **Cesar Chavez**. It now has about 100 000 members, mostly blacks, Mexican-Americans, and women.

Federal employees were given the right to organize and bargain collectively, but not to **strike**, by President **John F. Kennedy** in 1962. Many states followed suit and gave public employees the right to organize. The American Federation of State, County, and Municipal Employees became one of the fastest growing unions in the country. By 1987, this union had 1.1 million members.

Today, labour unions in the United States face a number of major problems. The decline of the traditional heavy or "smokestack" industries, such as iron and steel production, has meant a loss of jobs, the closing of plants, and reduced union membership. A second problem is foreign competition from the highly efficient industrial nations of southeast Asia, South Korea and Japan being two examples. Some of these newly industrialized nations pay low wages and offer few benefits to workers. This puts pressure on American businesses to cut costs by reducing wages and benefits. **Automation**, the greater use of industrial robots and computerization, has also contributed to job losses.

There is much criticism of unions in the United States. Some people claim that they are too big, inefficient, corrupt, and simply out-of-date. These people fail to appreciate the accomplishments of American unions. Table 6.7 shows the improvement in working conditions realized by American workers during the last century.

**Figure 6.11** *Cesar Chavez*

**Figure 6.12** *In this cartoon, management is supported by a corrupt government and an industry-subsidized press. The only weapon labour has is to strike, but it is plagued by poverty. How do you think the artist would have drawn the cartoon today?*

**Table 6.7** *Gains Made by the Labour Movement*

| ISSUE | 1880 | 1980 |
|---|---|---|
| Length of workday | 10 hours | 8 hours or less |
| Length of work week | 6 or 7 days | 5 days or less |
| Overtime pay | Almost none | At least 1.5 times normal |
| Paid vacations | Almost none | 2 to 4 weeks a year |
| Paid holidays | Almost none | 10 days a year |
| Hospital insurance | Almost none | Provided by employer |

## PROGRESS CHECK

1. **Compare the number of workers in farm and non-farm work in 1830 and 1980. What are some reasons for the changes that have taken place?**
2. **What percentage of workers in the United States are union members?**
3. **What do the abbreviations AFL and CIO stand for?**
4. **List some current problems facing the American union movement.**
5. **Refer to Table 6.7 and list the three improvements that you think are the most important. Give reasons for your choices.**

# Summary

How do government, business, and labour interact in the American market economy? Business seeks to create goods and services to satisfy the needs and wants of people; its goal is to make a profit. Labour provides workers to fill the jobs created by business. Labour unions attempt to get the maximum return for the efforts of the workers. The role of government in the United States is to provide the best conditions for both business and labour, using laws, regulations, and guidelines. These institutions interact with each other to provide a balanced economy that serves the needs of the American people.

# Checking Back

1. Look at Table 6.6 and determine which industries pay the highest wages today. Why do you think that this is the case?
2. Using the information from your chart (see page 67), write a short paper entitled, "The Role of Government, Business, and Labour in the American Market Economy." The paper should contain an introductory paragraph, a description of the role of each group, and a conclusion.

# Understanding Concepts

3. What does it mean to own shares in a corporation? How do shareholders influence the activities of their corporation?
4. Do a survey of your classmates to find out what occupations they prefer. Using this list, find out which occupations require union or association membership.

# Enrichment

5. Select a company you want to learn more about and write to the corporate office requesting a copy of their most recent annual report.
6. List the ten largest corporations from Table 6.2 and try to find out what products each business sells.
7. Sears, Roebuck and Company started as a mail-order business. What percentage of the company's profits comes from catalogue sales today?
8. Issue: Should professional athletes be allowed to form unions?
   Debate this issue, as a class or in small groups.
9. Compare the number of unionized workers in the United States with the number in Canada, United Kingdom, France, Sweden, Japan, and South Korea. List reasons to account for any differences in these numbers.

# SECTION III

# *The Market Economy of the United States*

Section I of this book dealt with the historical development of the American economy while Section II gave an overview of the country's economic geography. This background information helped you to understand the forces that influence the American market economy. Section III will focus on the theory and practice of the market economy in the United States, and investigate reasons why it functions as it does. The theory is explored in Chapter 7; Chapters 8 and 9 examine the role of the two key players in any market—the buyers and the sellers.

---

**SECTION III**
**Chapter 7:** The American Market Economy
**Chapter 8:** The Entrepreneur
**Chapter 9:** The American Consumer

---

As you study this section of the book, keep these questions in mind:
- What role do entrepreneurs and consumers play in the American market economy?
- What are some advantages and disadvantages of the market system as developed in the United States?

# CHAPTER 7

# *The American Market Economy*

**A**ll societies must answer the three basic economic questions:

(1) What goods should be produced?
(2) How should these goods be produced?
(3) For whom should the goods be produced?

There are different answers to these questions. For Americans, the answers might look like this:

(1) Produce the goods that I want to buy.
(2) Produce those goods that I want to buy in the most inexpensive way possible.
(3) Produce goods for those who are willing and able to pay for them.

These kinds of answers to the three basic economic questions are based on the belief that **consumers** know best. Consumers are people who buy **goods** or **services**. They make decisions to purchase certain products or services, and not others. Millions of individual consumer decisions create demands for particular things. **Producers** are the people who make and sell goods and services. They base their activities on what they think consumers demand. Buyers and sellers conduct their business in many places—in stores, service stations, offices, and so on. Taken together, these places of business are the **market**. In the market, consumers' needs are satisfied by producers' efforts. Understanding the concept of the market is key to learning how a market economy works.

**Figure 7.1** *All consumers make decisions about how to use their financial resources. Often, there are conflicts over what are the best uses.*

## FOCUS QUESTIONS

1. **What is a market economy? How does it work?**
2. **What are some advantages and disadvantages of the market economy?**
3. **How does the market economy of the United States compare with that of Canada?**

## CONCEPTS

economics
scarcity
resources
factors of production
traditional economy
centrally planned economy
market economy
demand line
supply line
equilibrium price

# Economics: The Science of Scarcity

**Economics** has been described as the science of **scarcity**. By definition, it is the science that investigates problems resulting from insufficient resources to satisfy human wants. The expression "human wants" includes both **wants** and **needs**. You might want a nice new car, but you do not need it. Needs are basic necessities, such as food, clothing, and shelter, while wants are those things that we desire.

In rich countries like the United States, wants and needs are often confused. Many things that were once considered wants are now needs— cars, electricity, radios, telephones, indoor toilets, hot showers, refrigerators, credit cards. Education was once thought of as a luxury for the privileged rich. Now, it is a necessity, of such importance that students are legally required to attend school to a minimum age. The same could be said about many other goods and services.

As a society's wants increase, more and more resources must be used to satisfy this demand. If each family wants two or three cars instead of one, then the supply of cars must increase to meet the demand. The same applies to the production of everything from telephones to shopping centres. *The basic rule of economics is that you cannot have everything.* Resources are limited, and they must be shared among all the people of the society.

There are many different ways for a nation to allocate resources. Each nation must decide how to accomplish this. One nation might choose to share the wealth equally while another may decide to let a few rich people get richer while millions starve. The method used is a product of the political, social, and economic forces within the nation.

**Figure 7.2** *Economic activity is based on the resources of land, labour, and capital.*

## Factors of Production

A **resource** is anything that can be used to create goods or services. Every society has three basic kinds of resources — **land**, **labour**, and **capital**. Land includes all the natural resources found in and on the land, such as forests, mineral deposits, oil, soil, natural gas, and water. These are sometimes called "gifts from nature" since we did not create them. The value of these natural "gifts" depends on their usefulness and scarcity. Gold is a precious metal that is hard to find, while sand is also useful but very easy to get. So, gold is much more valuable than sand.

Labour refers to human resources, including mental and physical labour. The architect who designs a house and the construction worker who builds it are examples of labour. The salesperson who sells the house and the entrepreneur who takes risks to develop the housing project are also examples of this factor of production.

Capital is money used to produce goods and services. It includes the money needed to pay for labour and the equipment used in the production of goods. Capital is created through the accumulation of wealth.

Economists call land, labour, and capital **factors of production**. In some cases, a fourth factor, called "entrepreneurship" is included; however, entrepreneurship is a special form of labour and can be included as part of that factor.

## - Organizing an Economy

In order for the resources of a society to be shared among the people, there must be some form of organization. Three basic ways to organize economies have been developed — traditional, centrally planned, and using market forces.

In a **traditional economy**, the three basic economic questions listed at the start of this chapter are answered by relying on what was done in the past. Customs and traditions are most important. For example, in the Middle Ages, the nobility were very rich while the peasants were very poor. By tradition, you were either born wealthy or poor and that is the way you remained for life. Similarly, in the traditional caste system of India, a person had to live and work within the role established for his or her social group. People born into the Untouchable caste could do only certain kinds of poorly paid labour, while those born into the Brahman caste became honoured priests with high social standing.

In a **centrally planned economy**, the three basic economic questions are answered by a central authority. This could be an absolute monarch, a dictator, or an elite group. The most common examples of central planning today are found in military dictatorships and communist governments. Some countries in Latin America are ruled by elite groups.

A **market economy** is a system where the collective economic decisions of individual buyers and sellers shape the economy of the whole country. In this system, buyers establish demands that sellers attempt to meet. Through give and take, buyers and sellers both meet their needs as best they can. There is no central authority to tell people what to produce or what to buy. The economy is run on the basis of individual decisions made by buyers and sellers.

## PROGRESS CHECK

1. **What are the three basic economic questions? What is the basic rule of economics?**
2. **Explain the difference between a need and a want. Give several examples of each.**
3. **Briefly describe the three factors of production.**
4. **In your opinion, which method of organizing the economy of a country would be most fair to the average person?**

# How the Market Economy Works

Of the three ways to organize a society, the United States has chosen to use the market economy. This method has strong similarities to American political ideals and the American tradition of the rights of the individual. *The American market economy has been described as a system where the economic decisions of individual buyers and sellers in the marketplace are used to make economic decisions for the whole country.*

Demand for a good or service is a fundamental part of the market economy. Figure 7.3 illustrates the demand for a particular product, in this case, records. Generally, if prices fall, demand rises, and vice versa. People are willing to buy more records if the price is low than if it is high. At a price of $16, people would buy only

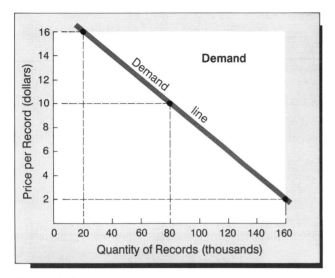

**Figure 7.3**

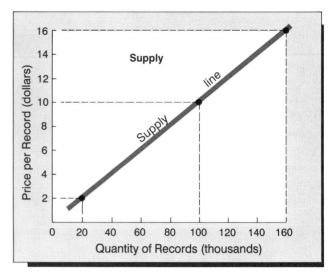

**Figure 7.4**

20 000 records. At $10, the demand would rise to 80 000 records, and if the price dropped to $2, the demand would be 160 000 records. When the points showing the amount demanded at each price are joined, the line that is created is the **demand line**.

Figure 7.4 shows the same product from the point of view of the seller. At $16, the seller is willing to supply 160 000 records because the profit would be very high. At $10, however, the seller is only willing to make 80 000 records. At $2, the quantity drops to 20 000. Generally, the higher the price, the greater the quantity the seller would like to make. The line connecting the points showing the quantity that would be produced at each price is called the **supply line**.

Now you have seen the market from the point of view of the buyers and of the sellers. Buyers want goods for the cheapest possible price while the sellers want to make the most money. In a market economy, this tension between buyers and sellers will always exist. In the end, both groups have to make trade offs. Buyers are forced to pay somewhat more than they would like to, and sellers have to sell for somewhat less than they want. The result is the **equilibrium price**, the

point where the demand and supply lines intersect. In the example, the demand and supply lines intersect at about $9, with a quantity of some 90 000 records.

## PROGRESS CHECK

1. **How is price set in the market?**
2. **By referring to the demand line, explain why some records go on sale for a reduced price.**

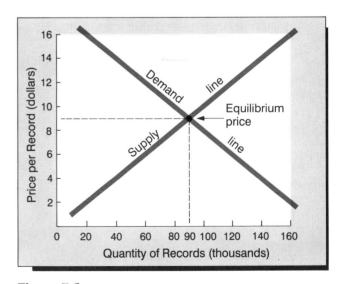

**Figure 7.5**

# Advantages and Disadvantages of the Market Economy

The question of advantage versus disadvantage depends on what values are considered important. In a market economy, **individual freedom** is very important. Consumers control the market by making choices about how they will spend money. If consumers demand more records, more records are produced. Likewise, as consumers demand more cars, the automobile industry churns out more cars. Sellers also have freedom. They make choices about what to make and how to go about selling it; thus, a big advantage of the market economy is the freedom for consumers to buy what they want, and for sellers to produce what will make the greatest profit.

Another advantage of the market economy is that it encourages **individual responsibility** in the marketplace. Those consumers who shop wisely and make good decisions get the best value. Sellers have to take responsibility for the products they make and sell. If consumers are not happy with the sellers' products or services, they will not spend their money where these products or services are sold. The choices that sellers make directly affect their success.

Perhaps the biggest advantage of the market economy is that it encourages **efficiency** and **innovation**. Consumers want the best value for their money and will try to shop wisely. Sellers compete with each other for the consumers' business. Sometimes sellers lower prices to make their products and services more attractive, but there are other strategies they can use to beat their competition. Many businesses work hard on improving their products in the hope that they will get a competitive edge over other sellers. Often, those companies that develop new technologies to improve products get the most sales, so market pressure constantly encourages the development of better products. Those businesses that are efficient and innovative do well, while those that are not face difficulties.

An important disadvantage of the market economy is the lack of planned direction and control of the economy. For example, should consumers be able to buy anything they demand? If consumers want handguns, firecrackers, liquor, or drugs without restrictions, should they be made available? Does it matter if people drive huge cars that waste fuel? Does it matter if some people waste their resources on luxuries while others lack basic necessities? These are difficult questions. To see some of the issues, examine the value judgements of these speakers.

**Figure 7.6** *Sellers compete against each other to get the consumers' business. This competition forces the sellers to be innovative.*

DEANA: If I want to spend my money on cars and clothes, that is my business. No one can tell me what I should or shouldn't buy. Government involvement should be very limited. I don't want some bureaucrat telling me I can't drive my four-wheeler up and down the country just because a few hikers don't like to see tire tracks or smell gasoline. Next thing they will do is pass some foolish law forcing me to quit smoking or wear a seat belt when I drive!

JAMIE: People can't just take off and do their own thing anymore. This isn't the Wild West with wide open spaces and few laws. We have to co-operate and plan things out for the good of all. The government must enforce laws that are in the best interests of society. We all know that smoking kills and seat belts save lives, so why not make laws that force everyone to quit smoking and wear seat belts? Of course, it is better to persuade people to do the right thing, but sometimes you simply have to make laws. Just because someone has a four-wheeler doesn't give him or her the right to tear up the countryside.

## PROGRESS CHECK

1. In one or two sentences, summarize each of the three advantages of a market economy.
2. Which of the two speakers would tend to be a supporter of a market economy? Explain your answer.
3. Which speaker's ideas do you support? Why?

## The Market Economies of Canada and the United States

The market economies of Canada and the United States have a similar history. Both nations value the idea of a free market; however, over time, the economies of the two nations have developed in different ways.

An important difference between the two market economies is that Americans tend to value the free market economy more highly than Canadians. The dream of starting with nothing and rising to the top is very strong in the United States. The ideal American is seen as a successful, self-made business person who succeeded because of talent and ambition. While this ideal is also present in Canada, it is not as strong.

The economy of Canada is usually described as a **mixed market economy** (see page 68). It has most of the features of the market economy but, since Canadians tend to accept more government involvement, there are also large, government-owned businesses such as Petro-Canada and the Canadian National Railway. These businesses were started in order to make sure that essential activities were developed in an organized way, rather than simply relying on market forces.

While the economies of both countries are similar, they are not the same. As you continue to study the American economy, you will be able to identify more of the similarities and differences. Perhaps by the end of this unit of study, you will have an opinion as to whether or not the Canadian economy should be more like the American economy.

# Summary

In this chapter, you have learned how a market economy works. A market economy is based on thousands of transactions between buyers and sellers. Prices are set for goods and services according to the supply and demand in the market. The advantages of the market economy have to do with freedom of choice and the encouragement of innovation and efficiency; the disadvantage is the lack of planning and control. There are similarities and differences between the economies of the United States and Canada, mostly having to do with the level of government involvement.

# Checking Back

1. Explain why economics has been called the science of scarcity.
2. Using your own words, describe each of the following:
   (a) traditional economy
   (b) centrally planned economy
   (c) market economy.
3. Explain how the price of an item is set in a market economy. Use graphs to help explain your answer.
4. Create three or four questions about the American or Canadian economy that you would like answered by an economist.

# Understanding Concepts

5. (a) Make a list of ten goods and services that you think are needs and ten that are wants. Share your list with others and, as a group, prepare a common list of needs and wants. Were there disagreements about the lists?
   (b) After your group has identified a list of needs and wants, try to establish criteria (reasons) to explain why certain items are needs while others are wants. Develop definitions for needs and wants.

6. Using the information in Table 7.1, create a supply and demand graph to find the equilibrium price for widgets (a mythical product often used as an example by economists). Use Figure 7.5 as a model for your graph.

**Table 7.1** *Supply and Demand for Widgets*

| QUANTITY DEMANDED | PRICE PER WIDGET | QUANTITY SUPPLIED |
|---|---|---|
| 160 | $1.00 | 20 |
| 140 | $2.00 | 40 |
| 120 | $3.00 | 60 |
| 100 | $4.00 | 80 |
| 80 | $5.00 | 100 |
| 60 | $6.00 | 120 |
| 40 | $7.00 | 140 |
| 20 | $8.00 | 160 |

# Enrichment

7. Study the free enterprise cartoon. What message is the artist trying to give the reader? What techniques did the artist use? Write your own humorous definition of the term "free enterprise".
8. Find out what a crown corporation in Canada is. Select one such corporation and try to find out why it was established.

**Figure 7.7**

# CHAPTER 8

# *The Entrepreneur*

In Chapter 7, you learned that the factors of production (land, labour, and capital) in the American market economy are allocated according to the demands of consumers. For example, if consumers want more compact discs, the demand goes up and the music industry produces more CDs. In this way, consumer demand spurs production.

Meeting the needs and wants of consumers is no simple task. Long-term planning is made difficult by the introduction of new **technology**. Technology includes both things and ideas. By definition, it is the science of technical processes applied to a field of knowledge. In an attempt to become more competitive, manufacturers are constantly developing new ideas and products. These new forms of technology very often stimulate other unexpected innovations. When the laser was invented, someone came up with the idea of using this new technology to make better sounding music recordings. This idea led to the development of the compact disc, which is a whole new way of recording and playing music.

Technological developments open up a whole new world of opportunities in any economy. In a market economy, however, it requires someone with entrepreneurial skills to take advantage of such opportunities. Thus, the entrepreneur plays an important role in supplying goods and services to meet consumers' demands.

## FOCUS QUESTIONS

1. What is an entrepreneur?
2. What are the major characteristics of an entrepreneur?
3. What role do entrepreneurs play in the market economy of the United States?

## CONCEPTS

technology              collateral

entrepreneur            venture capital

innovation              direct sales

franchise               commission

# The Characteristics of Entrepreneurs

The word **entrepreneur** comes from the French language and means a person who organizes and manages a business or enterprise and takes the risks associated with competing in a market economy. In a market economy, there are endless opportunities for new and improved products and services. The challenge is to put together the factors of production to compete successfully. This requires talent, skill, and a certain amount of luck.

To understand more about entrepreneurship in a market economy, look at some examples of American entrepreneurs. In the case of McDonald's Restaurants, **Richard** and **Maurice McDonald** started the business in San Bernardino, California, but it took the entrepreneurial skill of **Ray Kroc** to build the McDonald's empire. The second case study in this chapter is about **Stephen Wozniak** and **Steve Jobs**, co-founders of the Apple Computer Company. **Mary Kay**, an entrepreneur who created a successful business in personal care products, is the subject of the third case study.

## McDonald's Restaurants

McDonald's Restaurants is the largest and most successful fast-food chain in the world. In 1988, there were 10 000 restaurants worldwide. Well over 55 billion hamburgers have been sold by McDonald's. In the United States alone, McDonald's takes 20 percent of the $45 billion fast-food market and, with over 500 000 employees, is the single largest private employer in the country. One out of six restaurant visits in the United States is to McDonald's. All this began with a single restaurant opened by the McDonald brothers in 1937.

The McDonald brothers left New Hampshire in 1930 to seek work in California. They tried various businesses, but had their first success when they opened a small drive-in restaurant near Pasadena, California, in 1937. The brothers, nicknamed Dick and Mac, cooked the hot dogs (no hamburgers yet) and made milk shakes while three carhops took orders in the parking lot. In 1940, they opened a larger restaurant in San Bernardino, 80 km east of Los Angeles. Carhops on roller skates served up to 125 cars in the parking lot. The menu had 25 items and featured barbecued pork and beef sandwiches. McDonald's became the favourite hangout for teenagers in the area, and sales boomed.

McDonald's was not the first drive-in restaurant, nor the first one to serve hamburgers. The first known drive-in opened in 1932 in Hollywood. Other restaurants tried out different kinds of service and menu items to attract customers. In 1937, the Big Boy hamburger was introduced at **Bob Wian**'s drive-in near Los Angeles. It had two hamburger patties topped with sauces and vegetables and served on a triple-decker bun. This "sandwich" proved very popular and was quickly adopted by other restaurants, including McDonald's. At this time, there were dozens of drive-in restaurants in the Los Angeles area, so why did McDonald's do so well?

The McDonald brothers did some research and found that 80 percent of their business was in hamburgers. They decided to specialize in that item and drop the barbecued pork and beef sandwiches. The menu was then cut further from 25 items to 9—a hamburger, cheeseburger, three soft drink flavours, milk, coffee, potato chips, and pie. Later, French fries and milk shakes were added to the menu. The kitchen was changed so that everything could be cooked fast and served quickly. Paper products replaced glass and china dishes. The McDonald brothers described their business as a "Speedy Service System." To top it all off, the price of hamburgers was slashed from 30 cents to 15 cents.

Specializing in just a few items was a risky innovation. Most restaurants at the time offered a wide range of items to give customers more choice. The McDonald brothers sacrificed choice for speed and consistency. They explained, "If we give people a choice, there will be chaos." They were able to serve customers at a rate of five to six people per minute.

The McDonald brothers' innovation proved to be a success. It did to the fast-food industry what Ford had done to the automobile industry. The assembly line was designed for uniformity, efficiency, and high volume. At McDonald's, America got its first taste of the assembly line hamburger.

**Figure 8.2** *Edward H. Rensi, president of McDonald's U.S.A., watches Dick McDonald eat the 50th billion hamburger prepared by McDonald's Restaurants. This photograph was taken in November, 1984.*

**Figure 8.1** *The McDonalds renovated their restaurant in 1949, converting it from an ordinary carhop drive-in to a new fast-food restaurant.*

In a free market economy, a successful idea is always imitated by competitors. Surprisingly, the McDonald brothers openly shared the secrets of their success, willingly giving tours and detailed information to anyone who asked. This openness hurt their attempts to **franchise** their business. A franchise is a right to use a name or idea given by the owner for a fee. Why pay a franchise fee if you could simply go on a free tour and take notes?

In 1954, McDonald's was a small, successful drive-in restaurant. What it needed for further success was an entrepreneur with a big vision. Ray Kroc was such an entrepreneur. He took this small, local business and made it into an international fast-food giant.

Dick and Mac McDonald were inventors; Ray Kroc was a salesperson. He had worked as a salesperson for 25 years and had developed the sense of knowing what customers wanted. He also thought big. When he saw the McDonald brothers' drive-in, he knew that this idea had tremendous potential, even though he had never personally sold a hamburger; however, the brothers were basically local business people, content to make lots of money running a successful small business. They were not particularly interested in expanding across the nation.

**Figure 8.3** *Ray Kroc was the driving force behind the McDonald's Restaurant chain.*

It took some time, but eventually Kroc was able to convince the McDonalds to expand their business. At the age of 52, he began working for McDonald's as a franchise agent. Kroc was very aggressive and his company, McDonald's Corporation, Inc., began selling franchises across the country. It was his company that eventually created the McDonald's giant. A summary of developments shows what happened under Kroc's leadership.

**KEY DATES FOR McDONALD'S RESTAURANTS**

**1955** Kroc's first McDonald's franchise opens in Des Plaines, Illinois.

**1956** Kroc borrows $1.5 million to expand his company.

**1961** The McDonalds retire and sell all rights to Kroc for $2.7 million, most of which he had to borrow.

**1963** The double burger and cheeseburger are introduced.

**1965** McDonald's becomes a public corporation.

**1966** Ronald McDonald becomes the symbol for McDonald's Restaurants.

**1967** The first restaurant opens in Canada, on June 1, in Richmond, B.C. The menu had 10 items (see Table 8.1). Hamburgers now cost 20 cents.

**1968** Big Mac and the hot apple pie are introduced. The 1000th restaurant opens.

**1971** McDonald's Restaurants expand to Japan, Germany, and Australia.

**1972** The 2000th restaurant opens. Annual sales are over $1 billion.

**1973** Egg McMuffin is introduced.

**1974** The first Ronald McDonald House opens. The 15 billionth hamburger is sold.

**1975** The 10 000th student graduates from Hamburger University.

**1978** The 5000th store opens, in Japan. The 25 billionth hamburger is sold.

**1986** The 55 billionth hamburger is sold.

**1988** The 10 000th store opens. Sales are $60 billion.

**Table 8.1** *Menu at the First Canadian McDonald's Restaurant*

| | |
|---|---|
| Hamburger | 20¢ |
| Cheeseburger | 25¢ |
| French Fries | 20¢ |
| Hot Apple Pie | 25¢ |
| Milk Shakes | 20¢ |
| Milk | 15¢ |
| Coca-Cola | 10¢ and 15¢ |
| Orangeade | 10¢ and 15¢ |
| Coffee | 10¢ |
| Hot Chocolate | 10¢ |

## PROGRESS CHECK

1. **Who started McDonald's? When and where?**
2. **What innovations did the McDonald brothers try in order to make the restaurant more successful?**
3. **What happened to demand when McDonald's cut the price of their hamburger from 30 cents to 15 cents?**
4. **What is a franchise?**
5. **List all the reasons you can to explain why McDonald's Restaurants became so successful.**

### AN ISSUE: WHAT IS THE NUTRITIONAL VALUE OF FAST FOODS?

Ever since fast-food restaurants became popular, there has been an ongoing controversy as to the nutritional value of such food. Many health experts are concerned about the high levels of fat and "empty" calories in these meals. The issue flared up in 1988 when McDonald's opened eight restaurants in hospitals across the country.

Opposing the move was **Dr. Sidney Wolfe** of the Public Citizen Health Research Group, who spoke strongly against allowing such restaurants into hospitals. He claimed that fast foods " . . . significantly increase the risk of coronary artery disease and heart attacks." The American Heart Association was also alarmed. "We feel hospitals should provide leadership in health care," said spokesperson **Howard Lewis**. He

further complained that fast foods such as McDonald's are " . . . high in cholesterol, high in fat, and high in salt." **Dr. Virgil Brown**, also from the American Heart Association, stated: "Hamburgers are far and away the number one cholesterol problem in the country."

Supporting the move to allow fast-food restaurants in hospitals was **Dr. Michael Goldblatt**, McDonald's staff nutritionist. He defended the quality of the food served at McDonald's. "Our hamburgers contain no more than 22.5% fat. The restaurants offer food from the four groups. . . . It's possible to get a very light, nutritious meal. Our food is really no different than the kind of food you consume at home."

Table 8.2 shows the comparative nutritional value of a McDonald's meal with that of a "moral" meal. A moral meal is one that would be nutritionally good for you.

**Table 8.2** *Nutrient Value of a McDonald's Meal and a "Moral" Meal of the Same Basic Foods*

| NUTRIENTS | MCDONALD'S<br>QUARTER-POUND BURGER<br>FRENCH FRIES<br>APPLE PIE<br>VANILLA SHAKE | "MORAL"<br>QUARTER-POUND BURGER<br>BAKED POTATO<br>FRESH APPLE<br>SKIM MILK |
|---|---|---|
| Protein | 43 g | 40 g |
| Fat | 51 g | 25 g |
| Carbohydrate | 146 g | 90 g |
| Calcium | 446 mg | 365 mg |
| Sodium | 1476 mg | 1114 mg |
| Iron | 5 mg | 6 mg |
| Vitamin A | 263 I.U. | 650 I.U. |
| Niacin | 7 mg | 9 mg |
| Vitamin C | 14 mg | 40 mg |
| Calories | 1216 | 736 |

Now that you have briefly examined some data and opinions about the quality of fast foods, do you think that they are nutritious? Should these restaurants be allowed in hospitals?

# Apple Computers

The success of McDonald's Restaurants can be explained in economic terms. They are meeting the huge demand in the market for a good-quality, low-priced hamburger served quickly. Like McDonald's, the developers of the Apple computer also found a huge market. As you read this story, try to identify why Apple Computer, Inc. became so successful.

The earliest computers were huge, very expensive, and of limited use. They were used primarily by big businesses and governments. By 1974, however, the computer technology had advanced to the point where some small companies were selling primitive electronic kits to interested individuals. These kits sold for about $400, even though they had only 1K of memory. By the end of 1976,

**Figure 8.4** *ENIAC was the first electronic computer. Built in 1946, this computer used bulky vacuum tubes and filled a large room.*

**Figure 8.5** *Jobs and Wozniak with their Apple I computer in 1976*

there were six companies selling computer kits, with some 30 000 units sold. As the number of microcomputers increased, computer clubs were formed.

One such club near San Francisco was the Homebrew Club. It had about 500 members. One day in 1976, two members of the club, Stephen Wozniak and Steve Jobs, brought a computer they had built in their garage to a meeting. They could not afford to buy a kit, so they designed their own machine. Their invention was not just a kit, but a complete computer with a keyboard, a processor, 4K of memory, and an easy way to hook it up to a TV screen. And it all fit neatly in one box! The machine was called Apple I.

Stephen Wozniak (Woz) was the developer of Apple I. He was always interested in electronics and mechanical gadgets. At 13, he built a transistorized calculator that won him first prize in the Bay Area science fair. Woz tried a few years of college, but dropped out to work as a computer programmer for the Hewlett-Packard Company in Palo Alto, California. In 1971, Woz met another electronic hobbyist, Steve Jobs. Though Jobs was only 16 while Woz was 22, they became good friends. They were a natural pair. Woz was the technical expert while Jobs had the ideas. Like Woz, Jobs was also a school drop-out. He began working with the Atari video games company. Apple I was created by Woz in 1976 over a six-month period, with helpful ideas and parts supplied by Jobs.

Apple I was a big hit at the Homebrew Club. Woz took the machine to Hewlett-Packard and tried to convince them to produce it, but they simply were not interested in "toy" computers. The big computer companies thought that their market was in large, expensive business computers, not personal computers. Jobs, however, was convinced that the timing and technology were perfect for personal home computers that could help a small business or an individual. The market for a cheap personal computer would be enormous. When one of the Homebrew Club members ordered 100 Apple I computers for his store, Jobs knew that there was money to be made. Now the problem was to get the capital to buy the parts needed to make 100 computers!

Jobs and Woz bought parts on credit using their order for 100 Apples as **collateral**. In order to raise some cash, Jobs sold his Volkswagon bus and Woz sold the only thing he had of value, a programmable Hewlett-Packard calculator. This brought them $1350. They borrowed another $5000 from a friend and started building computers. Although the Apple I was a very simple computer, it was still more advanced than the competition's. The pair sold 175 at $666.66 a unit.

Woz created the Apple I machine, but Jobs created Apple Computer, Inc. They were two different types of entrepreneurs, one an inventor, the other a salesperson. While Woz concentrated on developing an even better computer, Jobs began to look for operating capital for the company. He tried to find a person to provide **venture capital** (money for new and very risky business ventures) for the new Apple Computer, Inc. To this end, he approached a 32-year-old millionaire named **A.C. Markkula**. Jobs showed Markkula Woz's new Apple II computer and convinced him to buy one-third of the company for $91 000. Jobs also got a line of credit from a bank for $250 000 and raised another $660 000 from friends and business acquaintances. Apple Computer, Inc. was now financially secure.

Apple became the fastest-growing business in American history. Sales skyrocketed. The large computer giants had missed a golden opportunity by not recognizing the potential demand for personal computers. Noting the phenomenal success of Apple, the computer giant IBM finally brought their own personal computer into the market in 1981, and sold 35 000 machines. In 1983, IBM sold 800 000 units. As Jobs had predicted, the demand for personal computers was enormous!

**THE FIRST YEARS OF APPLE COMPUTER, INC.**

**1976** Apple I computer created by Stephen Wozniak and Steve Jobs.

**1977** Apple II introduced for sale at $1195 with 16K memory. It was ideal for playing video games.

**1978** Apple sells 7600 computers.

**1979** Apple II Plus introduced, and 35 100 are sold. The Macintosh project begins.

**1980** Apple III introduced, and 78 100 are sold. Apple Computer, Inc. goes public.

**1981** IBM introduces a personal computer and sells 35 000 units. Apple sales reach $335 million, with 180 000 units sold.

**1982** Jobs appeared on the cover of *Time* magazine as one of "America's Risk Takers."

**1983** Lisa, Imagewriter, and Apple IIe are introduced. The one millionth Apple IIe is produced.

**1984** Macintosh and Apple IIc are introduced. Apple hits $1 billion in sales. The two millionth Apple IIe is sold.

**1985** Wozniak and Jobs receive the National Technology Award. Wozniak leaves Apple and starts a new company called CL9. Jobs resigns to form a new company, Next Inc.

**1986** Mac Plus is introduced. Jobs and Wozniak reach out-of-court settlement with Apple Computer, Inc. Jobs sells all but one of his shares in Apple Computer, Inc., making Markkula the largest single stockholder.

**1988** Jobs introduces the NeXT computer.

**1989** Jobs begins selling the NeXT computer.

**PROGRESS CHECK**

1. **Name the developers of the Apple computer. In what ways were these two individuals the same? different?**

2. **What is collateral? What collateral was used to raise money to build the first Apple computers?**

3. **Based on this case study, what would you consider the three most important characteristics of entrepreneurs?**

**Figure 8.6** *Apple Computer, Inc. continues to develop new products in order to stay competitive in the personal computer market.*

## Mary Kay Cosmetics

# MARY KAY

Mary Kay is a great-grandmother in her seventies. She believes strongly in free enterprise and feels that with a little hard work, anyone can achieve economic success in a free market economy.

In 1963, Mary Kay retired after a 25-year career in **direct sales** for a variety of companies. Direct sales involve having company representatives sell their products to customers in their own homes. There are many direct sales companies in the United States; one of the best known is the cosmetics company, Avon.

Mary Kay had encountered many problems in her career because she was a woman. She decided to write a book about these difficulties to help other women overcome the prejudice she had experienced in the workplace. After she got started, she realized that what she was really doing was drawing up a plan for a "dream company" that would allow women to have it all—a career that was financially rewarding and stimulating, as well as a strong family life. Instead of just writing about such a company, she decided to start one with all the characteristics that she felt to be important. The new company was founded in Dallas, Texas, in 1963 and was called Mary Kay Cosmetics.

Kay's two sons and daughter all helped her in her new venture. Richard gave up his job selling life insurance, took a cut in pay, and became financial director of the company. Ben handed over his life savings to create part of the "start-up" capital for the company. Eight months later, when his family circumstances permitted, Ben also gave up his job and joined the company as manager of the warehouse. Marylyn later became sales director. Their confidence in their mother paid off. At the end of the first year, company sales were $198 000; by the end of the second year, they had reached $800 000.

Mary Kay decided to concentrate on skin care products since this was a part of the market that was largely neglected by Avon. She believed that she could inspire ordinary women with little training in sales to go out and sell skin care products. Women would feel at ease selling these products to small groups in the customers' own homes. The company representatives would demonstrate the products by giving facial treatments, and the products would "sell themselves."

**Figure 8.7** *Mary Kay, chairperson of Mary Kay Cosmetics*

Women who sold products for Mary Kay were known as beauty consultants and they were paid a **commission** (a percentage of the price of each product sold). They were also paid a commission for recruiting new beauty consultants and received a percentage of the products sold by their new recruits. Kay says that she was not interested in the dollars-and-cents part of the business; rather, she wanted to offer women opportunities which did not exist elsewhere.

People thought that Kay's company was just too idealistic to work. Just like the bumblebee, whose body is too big for its wings, the company should never have been able to take off; however, just like the bumblebee, it achieved enormous success through hard work. The bumblebee became the symbol of success in the company and a diamond-studded bumblebee is one of the rewards given to Mary Kay consultants who achieve large sales volumes.

Another symbol of success — perhaps the best known one — is the pink Cadillac. Consultants who sell very large volumes of skin care products are given the privilege of using a pink Cadillac — a highly visible symbol of success!

Some women who have become national sales directors have been incredibly successful. A few earn salaries of hundreds of thousands of dollars a year and have become millionaires by selling Mary Kay products. Other consultants are less successful and may spend long hours earning little more than pocket money.

Mary Kay Cosmetics is still very much a family business. Mary Kay is the chairperson of the company and her son, Richard, is the president. She credits Richard with the business knowledge which has helped the company grow so quickly. There is no doubt that she has been one of the most successful entrepreneurs in recent years in the United States. Although there were many hard years at the beginning, the company has been extremely successful.

The company had a banner year in 1983 with over $300 million in sales and over $35 million in profits. At that point, there were almost 200 000 people selling Mary Kay products. Shortly afterwards, the company experienced some difficulties, and the number of salespeople declined to just over 152 000 and sales dropped to $278 million; however, by 1987, sales had rebounded to $326 million.

## PROGRESS CHECK

1. **Explain what is meant by direct sales.**
2. **How did Mary Kay finance her company?**
3. **Why did Kay concentrate on skin care products?**
4. **Explain what it means to be paid by commission. What do you think would be some advantages and disadvantages of being paid by commission rather than receiving a salary?**

**Figure 8.8** *Mary Kay rewards her successful sales directors with pink Cadillacs.*

# Entrepreneurs and Managers

Jobs and Wozniak saw an opportunity, took a risk, and became millionaires. Kroc saw an opportunity, gambled, and won. Mary Kay found a business opportunity in the skin care market. Throughout American history there are many such stories to tell. This is, after all, the American dream, the land of opportunity for those willing to take the risks.

One of the interesting questions that arises from both the Apple and McDonald's stories is why the originators did not last with the companies they created. The McDonald brothers sold their interest in the restaurant business to Kroc before it became a truly international success. Their dream was to retire as millionaires and enjoy life, a goal they realized. For Kroc, however, there was no such thing as enough success. His dream was to sell billions of McDonald's hamburgers around the world.

Jobs and Wozniak are good examples of entrepreneurs who were not good managers. They started from nothing and built an empire, but they lacked the skills to manage a large business empire. Running a corporation takes managers who make careful decisions to protect the investors. They tend to be conservative in their decisions and cautious about taking risks. Entrepreneurs are just the opposite. They are risk-takers and gamblers. They tend to win big, but they also lose big.

The story of the Apple computer is the dream of all would-be entrepreneurs — to get in on the ground floor of a new industry and watch it grow into a multibillion dollar company. The dream, however, has another side. There are always many more losers than winners. In a speech to the Edmonton Entrepreneurial Society, the veteran business person and politician **Nick Taylor** stated: "I have seen the ups and downs of my bank account through the years. So much so that I am convinced that all entrepreneurs will go broke eventually . . . " In the same speech, Taylor made an interesting distinction between entrepreneurs and managers: "Holding onto money, managing an operation, are management talents, but an entrepreneur is a different type of person." He listed a number of characteristics of an entrepreneur — determination, imagination, and the realization that the odds for success may be small, but the effort is worth it. An entrepreneur uses money rather than saves it. An entrepreneur cannot leave money in the bank. For them, Taylor claims: "Dollars are only good if they are out there working, doing something."

Mary Kay, on the other hand, is both an entrepreneur and a manager. Her many skills allow her to take risks and still keep the business operating efficiently. One of her greatest talents is the ability to motivate other people to perform their tasks to the best of their abilities. The success of others creates her success.

# Summary

In this chapter, you examined the important role played by entrepreneurs in the market economy of the United States. Americans have always viewed their country as a land of opportunity, a place where you can start with nothing and build a huge corporation. The entrepreneurial spirit is still alive and well in the United States, as you saw by studying various entrepreneurs — the McDonald brothers, Ray Kroc, Steve Jobs, Stephen Wozniak, and Mary Kay. By looking at these entrepreneurs, you were able to identify some major characteristics of innovators.

You were also able to contrast the characteristics of entrepreneurs and managers. Entrepreneurs tend to start things while managers keep the businesses going. Both are necessary in a market economy.

# Checking Back

1. Give reasons to explain why McDonald's Restaurants became so successful.
2. Explain the success of Apple Computer, Inc.
3. Suggest reasons to explain why Mary Kay Cosmetics has become a successful business.
4. List the major characteristics of an entrepreneur.
5. Describe the differences between an entrepreneur and a manager.

# Understanding Concepts

6. Imagine you are an entrepreneur attempting to start a new business.
   (a) Describe the product or service you plan to sell. What is your market? How much money do you think you could make?
   (b) How much capital do you need to start your business? How will you find this money?
   (c) Prepare a presentation of your business proposal as if you were going to try to convince a venture capitalist to lend you money. Make sure your presentation emphasizes your proposal's strengths.
7. Compare the beginnings of McDonald's Restaurants, Apple Computer, Inc., and Mary Kay Cosmetics in a chart with these headings: Year Started, Location, Financing, Problems.

# Enrichment

8. What is the success rate of new small businesses? Contact the local Chamber of Commerce, the Better Business Bureau, or find information in the library.
9. Do you know an entrepreneur? Select an entrepreneur from your local area and find out everything you can about that person's achievements. Write a report on your findings.
10. In 1954, several other fast-food franchise operators started, such as Kentucky Fried Chicken and Burger King. Other chains that started in the mid-1950s are Tastee Freeze, Dairy Queen, Big Boy, and Chicken Delight. Do research to find out what happened to these businesses. Prepare a short report and share this information with the class.
11. Research the life of entrepreneur J.P. Simplot, the potato king of Idaho, who is credited with inventing the "French fried" potato.
12. What is the current state of Apple Computer, Inc.? Is it growing? What new products does it now sell? If possible, compare this information to that of other computer companies such as IBM, Hewlett-Packard, UNISYS, Radio Shack, or Commodore.

# CHAPTER 9

# *The American Consumer*

Consumers create the demand in a market economy; businesses and entrepreneurs attempt to supply goods and services to meet the demands. It is important to understand the role of consumers in the American market economy because of the impact that they have. The collective decisions of consumers shape the economic activities of the nation.

## FOCUS QUESTIONS

1. **What is meant by consumer sovereignty?**
2. **How can consumers influence the market economy?**
3. **What rights and responsibilities do consumers have in the American market economy?**

## CONCEPTS

consumer sovereignty
consumers
advertising
fad

consumerism
rights
responsibilities

# Consumer Sovereignty

**Consumer sovereignty** describes the important role of consumers in a market economy. **Consumers** are the monarchs or sovereigns because of their power to buy goods and services. Their decisions affect the success of producers and sellers in the market. When enough consumers choose to buy a certain item, that item will continue to be made by the producers. Items that are not bought will eventually be dropped from the market.

In reality, it is more accurate to say that consumers *share* sovereignty. Consumer power depends on the number of consumers who are doing the same thing in a specific market. The purchase of one hamburger is quite insignificant, but when one million consumers buy the same kind of hamburger, the effect on the hamburger market is very powerful. Success or failure is determined by millions of individual decisions to buy or not to buy. In a sense, consumers use money to vote in favour of specific goods and services.

The idea that consumers are monarchs in a market economy has a long history. Prior to the Industrial Revolution, most goods and services were produced *after* consumers placed their orders. The goods were made for a specific customer. If someone wanted a pair of shoes, they went to a shoemaker and ordered a pair of shoes. Now, of course, customers simply go to stores and buy shoes made in some distant factory. Most goods and services today are produced *before* consumers decide to buy. Producers have to anticipate demand, guessing what goods and services consumers might want. Those who guess correctly succeed, while those who do not, fail.

In order to try to increase demand for their products, producers often use **advertising**. This is done to ensure that consumers have information about new products or services before they make their decisions.

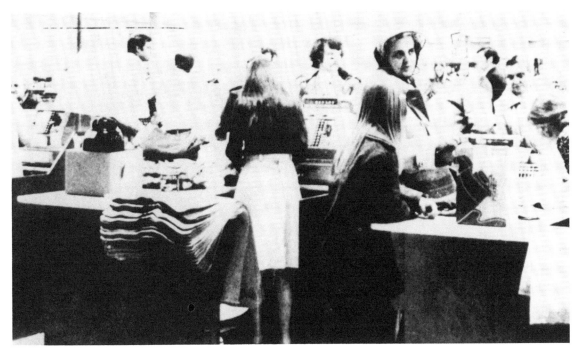

**Figure 9.1**

There is a debate about the role of advertising in a market economy. Does advertising create demand? Advertisers claim that only consumers create demand because consumers are free to buy or not to buy. Critics of advertising claim that consumers can be **manipulated** by advertising into buying goods and services they do not need. This is an important debate because if advertising can create demand, then consumers have lost some control of the market economy.

### A PROBLEM-SOLVING ACTIVITY: DOES ADVERTISING SERVE A USEFUL ROLE IN THE AMERICAN ECONOMY?

### Some arguments for advertising

- Advertising informs consumers about new products. Once the people are informed through advertising, they can make a choice to buy or not to buy.
- Advertising results in lower prices. By advertising products, producers can get more sales and improve the efficiency of the production process. Mass marketing means that each item is less expensive for individual consumers.
- Advertising gives consumers more choice. Consumers can compare products and select the most suitable for themselves.

### Some arguments against advertising

- Advertising can be misleading and can misinform customers. For example, the Ford Motor Company used to advertise that they had sold more "small" cars than any other company in the world. What the consumer was not told was that this claim was based on sales as far back as 1903. In this way, Ford implied that they made more small cars than Nissan, Mazda, or Toyota.
- Advertising can confuse consumers by making poor-quality products look good. The purpose of advertising is to sell, not to educate.

Advertisers highlight only the good side of a product and ignore the faults.
- Advertising encourages dissatisfaction and wasteful spending. Consider this quotation:

> Advertising . . . has no ethical goal and attempts only to produce the dissatisfied man, whose dissatisfaction can be cured— advertisers hope—by the purchase of specific products; dissatisfaction so that people will buy more.

> —S.I. Hayakawa, *US senator from California and former president of San Francisco State College*

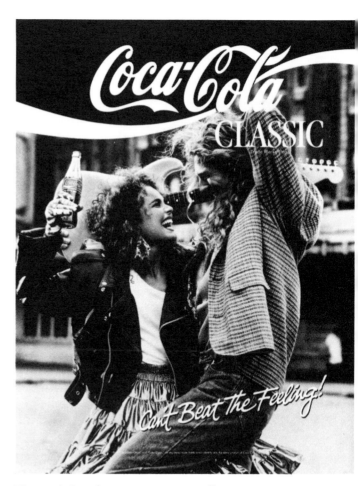

**Figure 9.2** *Advertising revenue allows magazines and newspapers to be sold for very inexpensive prices.*

Use these steps to develop your own conclusions about this problem.

(1) Identify the problem by giving your understanding of what the problem is.

(2) Summarize arguments for and against the question.

(3) Gather additional information from other sources.

(4) Decide which alternative you support and list arguments to back up your decision.

## PROGRESS CHECK

1. **What is meant by the term "consumer sovereignty"?**

2. **Write a short essay outlining the advantages and disadvantages of advertising.**

## The Role of Consumers

In 1989, there were 247.5 million people in the United States and, therefore, that number of consumers. As citizens of one of the wealthiest countries of the world, Americans have a great deal of purchasing power. When consumers spend their money, they determine the demand for specific goods and services, which producers try to meet. You saw in Chapter 8 how the demand for personal computers provided a growing market for the Apple computer along with others, such as Commodore, Atari, and IBM. Similarly, the demand for fast-food hamburgers created a huge market for sellers like McDonald's, Dairy Queen, Wendy's, and others. It was consumer interest in personal computers and fast-food hamburgers that allowed the success of these companies. And, of course, if consumers decide they no longer want these goods, companies will either disappear or start making and selling something else. In a market economy, the demand by consumers determines which companies succeed or fail.

It is general consumer interest that determines the kinds of goods and services available at any particular time. If there are not enough people wanting a good or service, sellers will not make it available. There are thousands of examples of goods and services that were once in high demand but are now forgotten. The hula hoop, miniskirt, and drive-in theatre are a few examples. Can you think of other items that were once popular but are now either fading in popularity or have disappeared completely?

### CASE STUDY: THE HULA HOOP

A hula hoop craze started in California in the spring of 1957. Two entrepreneurs, **Spud Melin** and **Richard Knerr** of the Wham-O Company, heard about hoops while attending a toy fair in New York. The wooden hoops they saw were used in Australian schools for gymnastics. Melin and Knerr started to make some and personally sold them to youngsters in parks and schools. But the wooden hoops were heavy and not very flexible and were not successful. Later, Melin and Knerr started to make them out of plastic, and interest in the hoops began to grow.

The new hoops were plastic rings about 1 m in diameter. The challenge of the hoop was to try to keep it turning around your waist for as long as possible. One 10-year-old boy from New Jersey set a record of 3000 spins. The name hula hoop came from the body motions that were used, actions similar to the movements of the hula dancers in Hawaii. The hula hoop craze caught on and the Wham-O Company was making 20 000 hoops per day to meet the demand. The hoops cost about 50 cents to make and sold for $1 to $2 each. At the peak of the craze, 40 different companies were making and selling hula hoops. By the end of 1958, some 15 million hoops had been sold.

The hula hoop fad did not last. Demand dropped just as quickly as it grew. Hula hoops can still be found today because they are an inexpensive toy, but demand is only a small part of what it was during the height of the hula hoop craze.

## PROGRESS CHECK

1. **Why are consumers such an important group in the economy?**
2. **What is a fad? Can you identify some recent fads?**

**Figure 9.3** *Hula hoops enjoyed great popularity for a brief time. Why do some items cause fads, but not others?*

# Consumer Issues in the American Market Economy

**Consumerism** became popular in the 1960s. It was a movement similar to others at the time, including the civil rights and peace movements. The most famous consumer advocate was **Ralph Nader** who published a book in 1966 called *Unsafe At Any Speed*. He documented the poor safety record of the automobile industry. In particular, Nader showed how General Motors' Corvair was dangerous "at any speed" and the cause of many deaths.

What Nader and other consumer advocates wanted were government regulations to control producers. They claimed that producers were simply interested in profits, not public safety; thus, industries must be forced to make safer products and eliminate harmful pollution. Producers, on the other hand, were strongly opposed to more government involvement in the market economy. They claimed that they voluntarily maintained high standards and never deliberately built dangerous products or damaged the environment. Producers argued that they responded to consumer concerns. If consumers value safety and protection of the environment then producers would change their behaviour to meet this demand. That, they argued, is the way things are done in a free market economy.

A retired chairperson of General Motors suggested that the real aim of consumer advocates was to drive a wedge between consumers and producers, to undermine the good relationship that always existed between the two groups. Some producers even claimed that consumer groups were attacking the whole idea of free enterprise and promoting socialism. Consumer groups argued it is only fair that consumers in a free market should organize to force producers to make better goods and services. What do you think of these arguments?

The result of the consumer movement of the 1960s and 1970s was the passage of many regulations by Congress. These are some of the more important laws:

- Truth in Lending Act;
- Fair Packaging and Labeling Act;
- Wholesome Meat Act; and
- Magnuson-Moss Warranty Act.

The United States Federal Trade Commission has compiled the following statistics showing estimates of the benefits of health and safety regulations:

- safety packaging resulted in a 40 percent reduction in child poisoning;
- higher safety standards for baby cribs led to 50 percent fewer deaths and 45 percent fewer injuries; and
- federal government vehicle safety regulations saved 28 000 lives between 1966 and 1974.

## PROGRESS CHECK

1. **When did the consumer movement begin? Why did it start?**
2. **What did consumer advocates like Ralph Nader want governments to do?**
3. **Describe the attitudes of producers toward consumer groups. Why do you suppose they are opposed to more government regulations?**

**DANGER**
POISON   EXTREMELY FLAMMABLE
DIRECT INHALATION OF SPRAY MAY BE HARMFUL
CONTAINER MAY EXPLODE IF HEATED

**Figure 9.4**

SURGEON GENERAL'S WARNING: Smoking Causes Lung Cancer, Heart Disease, Emphysema, And May Complicate Pregnancy.

## Rights and Responsibilities of Consumers

Many American consumer **rights** were formalized by President **John F. Kennedy** in 1962. A series of consumer laws were passed outlining four basic rights. These are the rights to:

- safety;
- information;
- choice; and
- be heard.

The right to safety led to laws to regulate such goods as food, clothing, drugs, cosmetics, and car tires. Laws supporting the right to be informed were directed against false advertising and for true interest rates and proper labels showing ingredients and nutritional value of food products. The right to choose deals with antitrust legislation to avoid **monopolies**. Having the right to be heard means that consumers have the freedom to express their concerns. This has resulted in the creation of special government agencies to promote consumer concerns. Governments in the United States responded to consumer pressure because consumers are also voters. Consumers as a group can make changes through their elected politicians.

Laws to protect consumers are examples of government involvement in the marketplace. If cars must have expensive safety equipment or meet high pollution standards, then the price of cars will be higher. Consumers have no choice but to pay the higher prices. At times, some people will object to laws designed to protect consumers generally. For example, many people do not like to wear seat belts in automobiles or helmets when riding motorbikes; however, in a democratic society such as the United States, there are **responsibilities** as well as rights. *A responsible citizen must have respect for all laws, not just the ones he or she likes.*

## The Need For Balance

The need for government regulation of some aspects of the American market economy must be balanced by the desire for less government involvement. This question of balance was addressed in 1980 by **Harold Williams**, chairperson of the United States Securities and Exchange Commission, who argued that the government has a role to play in the market economy. He said that " . . . private economic power must be accountable to the public good."

From 1980 to 1988, under the Republican administration of President Ronald Reagan, consumer rights were de-emphasized. The conservative politics of the Reagan administration favoured reducing the role of government in the marketplace. Budgets for consumer advocate programs were slashed, but many of the regulations developed in the 1960s and 1970s remained in effect.

In a free and democratic society, consumers have a responsibility to exercise good judgement. If they shop wisely, poor products and services should not survive in a free market. Unscrupulous producers and inefficient business people will not last for long if consumers exercise their best judgement.

## Summary

This chapter examined consumer sovereignty and the role that consumers play in the American market economy. Some problems facing consumers were examined, specifically the need for government intervention to maintain high safety and pollution standards. Finally, the rights and responsibilities of the consumer were outlined.

## Checking Back

1. (a)  In what ways do individual consumers influence the market economy?
   (b)  In what ways have consumer groups influenced the market economy?
2. Identify and explain the rights and responsibilities of consumers in the American market economy.

## Understanding Concepts

3. Which group has the most control over the type and price of goods and services, consumers or producers? Study the points of view below and decide which one you agree with. Are there other arguments you could add? When you have completed your study, write a short position paper on this topic.

*Some arguments in favour of consumer control*
- Consumers are free to buy what they want. Sellers cannot force anyone to buy something. Consumers only get what they want.
- Consumers will shop wisely for the best and cheapest product or service; therefore, only the best and lowest-priced items will survive in a free market.
- Consumers have political power. They are voters so they can get their elected government to force changes on producers if necessary.

*Some arguments in favour of producer control*
- Producers are usually a small group so they can easily get together to set any price they want; that is, they can form a **monopoly**.
- Producers can use advertising in the mass media to create wants and needs in consumers. This

advertising can mislead or confuse consumers to buy goods or services they do not need.

• Producers have political power. Politicians will tend to listen more to a few rich producers than a large group of poor and disorganized consumers.

# Enrichment

4. Compare television or magazine ads for a product with an objective evaluation from consumer groups. *Consumer Report* is a good place to find unbiased tests. How do the advertisements compare with the reports?

5. Should governments set minimum safety standards to protect consumers? Based on your reading in this chapter, plus additional research, write a short paper outlining your position on this question.

6. Analyze the following two statements about the role of advertising in the American market

economy. The following steps are suggested.

(a) Identify the central idea in each statement. Express that idea in your own words.

(b) Determine the point of view taken by each of the authors.

(c) Decide if you agree or disagree with these statements. Give reasons for your opinions.

### Statement A

Excessive and inflated advertising claims are more "subversive" of the capitalist system than any amount of radical propaganda and more effective, too, in creating cynics and unbelievers out of young children who quickly learn to distrust Establishment voices.

–**Sydney Harris**, *nationally syndicated columnist*

### Statement B

It is television advertising which has made Madison Avenue the arch-symbol of tasteless materialism.

–**David Ogilvy**, *president of his own advertising company*

# Life Today in the United States

Section I of this book examined historical forces that led to the industrial development of the United States. Section II described the geography of the United States and its effect on the present-day economy. The roles of the country's major institutions — government, business, and labour — were explained. In Section III, the internal workings of the market economy were investigated, along with the roles played by consumers and entrepreneurs. This section focusses on the quality of life enjoyed by people in the United States. In general, Americans have applied the basic principles of the market economy to create enormous wealth and abundance, but the creation of wealth has caused problems.

Chapter 10 looks at how industrial growth has had a harmful impact on the environment, while important issues related to the distribution of wealth are discussed in Chapter 11. America is seen as the land of opportunity, but many Americans do not have equality of opportunity. The final chapter deals with the future of the American economy and society.

### SECTION IV

**Chapter 10:** Environmental Issues
**Chapter 11:** Economic Values and the Quality of Life
**Chapter 12:** Looking into the Future

As you study this section of the book, keep this question in mind
- How has the quality of life been shaped by economic growth in the United States?

# CHAPTER 10

# *Environmental Issues*

The year 1776 is especially significant for the American people for two very different reasons. One reason is that the Declaration of Independence was signed in that year. The other reason, less well known, is that this was the year that **Adam Smith** published his book, *The Wealth of Nations*.

Smith is known as the "founder of economics." He outlined the basic theory of the market economy, arguing that the best economic system is one with a free market and very little government interference. The best government, he maintained, was the least government. His ideas are still the bedrock of the American market economy.

But in a market economy, who will look after the public good? Who will care for the poor, maintain public facilities, protect consumers, and ensure fairness in the marketplace? Adam Smith's answer was the "**invisible hand**." He believed that people will naturally do what is best because of self-interest. This self-interest should cause producers to develop the best products and services, and consumers to shop wisely. The overall general effect would be to improve society. The material welfare and **quality of life** for both consumers and producers should rise. There would be no need for "visible" or direct government rules because the market economy would automatically look after the interests of the people.

One criticism of the "invisible hand" theory is the assumption that everything is done for purely economic reasons; thus, for example, business owners will pay fair wages because this keeps employees working, not because it is the right thing to do. Employees will work hard to keep their jobs because of the pay, not because of the satisfaction of working. In fact, economics is only one part of people's lives. Often people are motivated by other things. They give money to build a park to create more beauty, not just to increase property values. Restaurant servers smile at customers as a sign of friendship and not just to get a bigger tip. Smith's theory did not adequately take into account the wide range of values that people have.

The basic values that underlie the market economy need to be examined. One of these values is the need for economic growth. Workers want higher wages and businesses want higher profits. But what price are people willing to pay to maintain constant economic growth?

**Figure 10.1** *Adam Smith, the founder of economics*

This question is important because of competing values in society. Many people prefer a clean environment over constant economic growth and development. They question the purpose of life. Is it simply to make and spend money, or is it to make a better world? To many, quality of life is based on many values, including economic growth, social justice, fairness, respect for the environment, and respect for others.

In this chapter, misuse of the environment will be used as a case study to illustrate competing values. The current environmental problems of the United States are so serious that the combined efforts of industry, government, labour organizations, and individual citizens are needed for any hope of success. This shows that the public interest is not completely served in a market economy by the "invisible hand." How Americans deal with this issue gives us a good insight into the workings of the American market economy.

## FOCUS QUESTIONS

1. **What role do government, business, and individual citizens play in solving problems in the United States?**
2. **What impact does economic growth have on the quality of life?**
3. **Who looks after the public interest in the American market economy?**

## CONCEPTS

| | |
|---|---|
| **"invisible hand"** | **greenhouse effect** |
| **quality of life** | **recycling** |
| **public good** | **lobby groups** |
| **pollution** | |
| **solid wastes** | |
| **lead pollution** | |
| **acid rain** | |

# Pollution

**Pollution** is a problem in all societies. Wherever people live, they have an impact on the environment. Industrialized nations such as the United States create a great deal of environmental damage through economic activities. Many by-products of industries — nuclear wastes and chemical pollutants to name two — are particularly dangerous. In this chapter, the general term "pollution" will be used to refer to all forms of damage to the environment. Land, air, and water pollution in and around the United States will be examined.

## Land Pollution

The land is polluted when we dump our **solid wastes** into the environment. Municipal solid wastes are produced in homes, restaurants, office buildings, industrial sites, and the like. Industrial solid wastes are by-products of manufacturing processes.

There are two common methods used in the United States for getting rid of solid wastes — landfill and incineration. Landfill sites are commonly called garbage dumps. Some of these are unsightly, open dumps, while others are properly operated sanitary landfills where each layer of waste is covered over with dirt. After a sanitary landfill site is full, it can be covered over, planted with grass, and used for recreation purposes. This is a very clean and effective way to get rid of garbage. The drawback is that it requires a good deal of land, and sites are expensive to maintain.

Locating landfill sites is often very controversial. Communities usually want them close enough to keep transportation costs to a minimum, while residents want them located as far as possible from their homes. Debates over the choice of sites can be quite bitter.

**Figure 10.2** *Protestors demonstrating in Vernon, near Los Angeles, about a decision to build an incinerator in their town*

An alternative method of disposal is incineration. Wastes are fed into incinerators and the remaining ash—only a small portion of the original volume—is dumped in landfill sites; however, this can cause air pollution. Improper burning releases poisonous gases and harmful particles into the atmosphere. Figure 10.2 shows citizens protesting the building of an incinerator at Vernon, an industrial city 5 km from downtown Los Angeles. The incinerator was built despite the protest.

## Air Pollution

Figure 10.3 gives information about the five major types of air pollution and their sources. Air pollution is a mixture of harmful gases and **particulates** which have been released into the atmosphere. Particulates are small particles of liquid or solid matter.

Air pollution harms the health of people, especially those with respiratory illnesses. It kills plant life and causes extensive damage to buildings over time.

Forty-two percent of the air pollution in the United States is caused by transportation activities. The automobile is the single greatest

**115**

polluter in the country. Other major sources are solid waste incinerators and electric power generating stations that burn fuels such as coal. Only eight percent of pollution comes from natural sources like forest fires.

Emissions from motor vehicles contain nitrogen oxides and lead. **Lead pollution** is particularly dangerous because it accumulates in the environment. In an effort to reduce lead pollution, the government passed laws requiring car manufacturers to produce vehicles using unleaded gasoline. The vehicles also had to have other devices designed to control pollution. It has been estimated, however, that one in ten automobile owners in the United States uses leaded fuel illegally because it is cheaper. This problem may soon be solved permanently as many countries have now set deadlines for the complete elimination of leaded gasoline.

Forcing people to use unleaded gasoline is an example of government intervention in the market economy to ensure a public good. From an economic point of view, this action did not make sense; however, from an environmental point of view, it was necessary. The government was caught in the middle of competing values. If nothing was done, environmental pollution would continue, but laws forcing manufacturers to add pollution controls made cars more expensive. As the price of cars goes up, demand goes down, and workers are laid off. The effect of the government intervention is a cleaner environment, but unemployed workers are certainly not happy and neither are consumers who must pay more for cars. If Adam Smith had been right, car manufacturers and consumers would have naturally decided to use unleaded fuel to protect the environment. The "invisible hand" seldom works in practice, so governments must make and enforce laws and regulations.

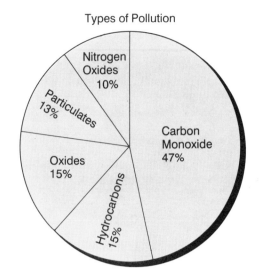

Types of Pollution

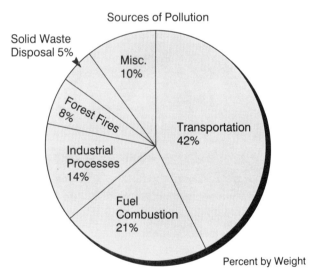

Sources of Pollution

Percent by Weight

**Figure 10.3** *Air pollution in the United States*

## PROGRESS CHECK

1. **Explain what Adam Smith meant by the term "invisible hand".**
2. **Suppose you are the mayor of a community considering building an incinerator. List the pros and cons that you would need to think about before you make up your mind.**
3. **What is the single greatest cause of air pollution in the United States?**

**116**

# Acid Rain

**Acid rain** is a form of air pollution produced by emissions of sulphur dioxide ($SO_2$) and nitrogen oxides ($NO_X$). The main sources of sulphur dioxides are coal-burning power generating stations; nitrogen oxides come mainly from automobiles. These substances combine with water in the atmosphere to form sulphuric and nitric acids. These acids return to the earth's surface as rain, snow, and smog.

Acid rain damages the environment in many ways. When it falls on lakes, it increases their acid content, killing plant and fish life. Thousands of lakes are now considered dead because of acid rain. Acid rain affects more than just lakes, though. It also damages trees, crops, and soils, and erodes public buildings and statues.

Emissions causing acid rain could be reduced through stricter pollution controls. The problem, of course, is that it would cost a great deal of money. In the early 1980s, it was estimated to cost between $2.5 and $4 billion to reduce emissions by 50 percent. Who should pay for this? Private companies argue that they cannot afford expensive "scrubbing" equipment for smokestacks. American citizens do not want higher taxes to pay for the equipment. Until recently the United States government has argued that the problem is not serious enough to justify the high costs; however, they have now proposed legislation to control the pollution.

Figure 10.4 shows that much of the acid rain generated in the United States is swept by winds into Canada. Attempts by the Canadian government to deal with the problem have met with little success. As long as acid rain is carried northward over the border, damage in Canada will continue.

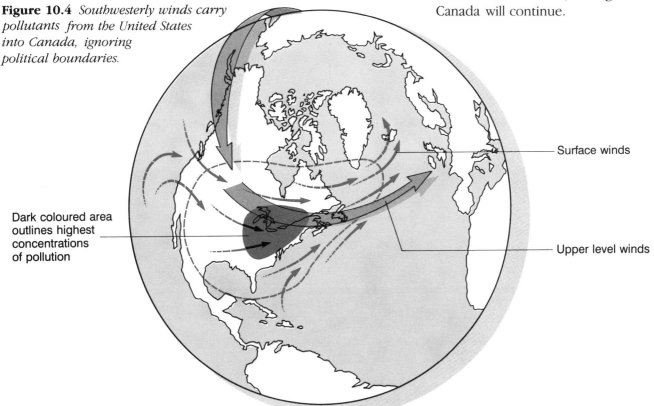

**Figure 10.4** *Southwesterly winds carry pollutants from the United States into Canada, ignoring political boundaries.*

Dark coloured area outlines highest concentrations of pollution

Surface winds

Upper level winds

# The Greenhouse Effect

Air pollution is changing global weather patterns. Carbon dioxide emissions from the burning of vegetation and fossil fuels have produced the **greenhouse effect**.

Carbon dioxide acts like the glass in a greenhouse, trapping radiation from the sun and preventing it from being lost back to space. This has resulted in a gradual increase in the world's temperature and changes to the earth's weather patterns. These changes in the global environment could have a serious effect on the whole planet, including large-scale climatic change and the melting of ice caps.

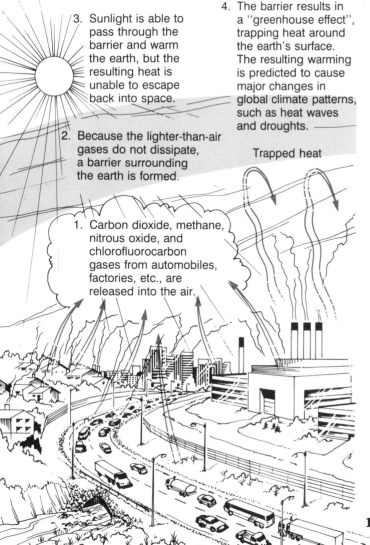

3. Sunlight is able to pass through the barrier and warm the earth, but the resulting heat is unable to escape back into space.

4. The barrier results in a ''greenhouse effect'', trapping heat around the earth's surface. The resulting warming is predicted to cause major changes in global climate patterns, such as heat waves and droughts.

2. Because the lighter-than-air gases do not dissipate, a barrier surrounding the earth is formed.

Trapped heat

1. Carbon dioxide, methane, nitrous oxide, and chlorofluorocarbon gases from automobiles, factories, etc., are released into the air.

**Figure 10.5** *The greenhouse effect*

# Water Pollution

The marine explorer, Jacques-Yves Cousteau, has stated: ''The very survival of the human species depends on the maintenance of an ocean clean and alive . . . .'' Yet in 1988, more than 80 km of New York City and Long Island beaches were declared temporarily off limits for swimming because of pollution. Beaches in Rhode Island and Massachusetts were polluted by medical wastes and untreated sewage. Fishing boats off the eastern seaboard have been catching fish with ugly, ulcerous lesions and rotting fins. Poisonous blooms of algae, known as red and brown tides, frequently affect coasts and bays of the United States, contaminating fish and crustaceans.

Off the Atlantic Coast and in the Gulf of Mexico are huge zones of **anoxic water**, water depleted of oxygen. This is caused by the decay of algae. The rotting vegetation uses up oxygen in the water causing fish and other organisms to die. In the early summer of 1988, one million fluke and flounder were killed when they were trapped in anoxic water.

The West Coast of the United States is also heavily polluted. For example, the bay off Seattle is contaminated with a variety of industrial chemicals, such as copper, lead, zinc, arsenic, cadmium, and PCBs. These have been deposited in layers on the bottom of the bay. Figure 10.6 shows the various sources of pollution along the United States coasts.

Commercial fishing in the United States generates $3.1 billion every year. This industry is seriously threatened by coastal pollution. Contaminated fish have diseases such as gastroenteritis, hepatitis A, and cholera. Pollution kills as many as two million seabirds and 100 000 marine mammals every year.

In the United States, more and more people now live near the coasts. Between 1940 and 1980, the number of Americans living within 80 km of a

**118**

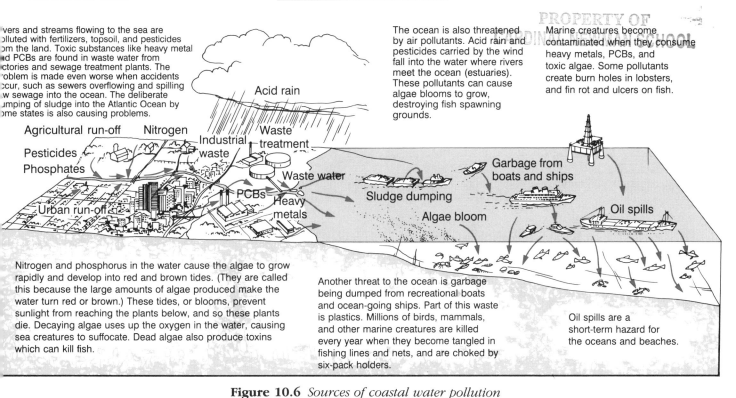

ivers and streams flowing to the sea are olluted with fertilizers, topsoil, and pesticides om the land. Toxic substances like heavy metal d PCBs are found in waste water from ctories and sewage treatment plants. The oblem is made even worse when accidents ccur, such as sewers overflowing and spilling w sewage into the ocean. The deliberate mping of sludge into the Atlantic Ocean by ome states is also causing problems.

The ocean is also threatened by air pollutants. Acid rain and pesticides carried by the wind fall into the water where rivers meet the ocean (estuaries). These pollutants can cause algae blooms to grow, destroying fish spawning grounds.

Marine creatures become contaminated when they consume heavy metals, PCBs, and toxic algae. Some pollutants create burn holes in lobsters, and fin rot and ulcers on fish.

PROPERTY OF CARDINAL NEWMAN SCHOOL

Acid rain

Agricultural run-off  Nitrogen

Pesticides
Phosphates

Industrial waste

Waste treatment

Waste water

PCBs

Heavy metals

Urban run-off

Garbage from boats and ships

Sludge dumping

Algae bloom

Oil spills

Nitrogen and phosphorus in the water cause the algae to grow rapidly and develop into red and brown tides. (They are called this because the large amounts of algae produced make the water turn red or brown.) These tides, or blooms, prevent sunlight from reaching the plants below, and so these plants die. Decaying algae uses up the oxygen in the water, causing sea creatures to suffocate. Dead algae also produce toxins which can kill fish.

Another threat to the ocean is garbage being dumped from recreational boats and ocean-going ships. Part of this waste is plastics. Millions of birds, mammals, and other marine creatures are killed every year when they become tangled in fishing lines and nets, and are choked by six-pack holders.

Oil spills are a short-term hazard for the oceans and beaches.

**Figure 10.6** *Sources of coastal water pollution*

**Figure 10.7** *Pollution trouble spots on America's coasts*

Wash.

Oreg.

Calif.

Maine

N.H.

Mass.

R.I.

Conn.

N.J.

N.Y.

Del.

Md.

Va.

N.C.

S.C.

Miss.   Ala.   Ga.

Texas

La.

Fla.

Gulf of Mexico

▼ High levels of toxic chemicals in fish livers

● PCB or pesticide contamination

○ Areas of oxygen depletion

■ Areas in which more than one-third of acreage is closed to commercial shellfish harvest

0        400        800 km
Scale

**119**

coastline more than doubled, from 42 million to 89 million. The huge amounts of domestic and industrial pollutants generated by so many people is overwhelming even the oceans' great capabilities to recover. The United States **Environmental Protection Agency** (EPA), an independent agency of the federal government concerned with protection of the environment, has been criticized because less than ten percent of the more than 5000 types of wastes considered dangerous are now being regulated.

In 1972, the United States federal government passed the **Clean Water Act**, setting pollution standards for water. Because of the expense, some cities, such as Boston, will not be able to comply with the minimum standards set down in this act until 1999. There are people in the United States who believe that the government should not interfere in the marketplace by passing such laws. But there are many who want the government to continue to set rules to promote a cleaner environment. In recent years, the United States has spent about $100 billion on cleaning water discharges from factories and cities. In spite of these enormous amounts, problems continue.

There are some success stories in the fight against water pollution. The Delaware River estuary has almost six million people living close by. In recent years, efforts at pollution control have greatly improved this area. Over 33 species of fish which had all but vanished have now returned, including the shad fish which had been absent for over 60 years.

## PROGRESS CHECK

1. **What is acid rain? What are the effects of acid rain?**
2. **What is the "greenhouse effect"?**
3. **What are the sources of water pollution? What is being done to improve the situation?**

# The Causes of Pollution

Technological advances in agriculture, industry, and transportation have often had harmful environmental side effects. The use of fertilizers and pesticides in agriculture has increased the problems of pollution from run-off. **Rachel Carson**, in her famous book *Silent Spring*, described the harmful effects of pesticides such as DDT. DDT was used widely until its harmful effects became known. Now it is banned in the United States and many other countries.

High-compression automobile engines were developed to meet the demands of consumers for more powerful automobiles. Unfortunately, these engines required the use of additives in their gasoline, such as lead; thus, the problem of lead air pollution was brought about by consumer demand and the response by producers to meet that demand. As so often happens, the harmful effects of new technologies only become apparent after damage has occurred.

Technology creates environmental problems, but it can also be used to solve problems. Smaller, cleaner automobile engines have been developed and safe fertilizers and pesticides are available. New biodegradable plastics are beginning to be used in place of older, harmful products.

Most pollution problems exist because methods of preventing pollution are expensive. For example, sulphur in the form of sulphur dioxide is released into the atmosphere when coal is burned. In the United States, about 18 million tonnes of sulphur dioxide is released every year in this way. This amount happens to be almost exactly the amount of sulphur that American industries need. Most of the sulphur in the sulphur dioxide could be recovered and used by the sulphuric acid manufacturers, but as yet there is no practical, inexpensive way of doing this.

Much of the pollution in the United States and other industrialized countries is a result of the need to save time, effort, and money. Preventing pollution is often just too inconvenient. The use of disposable products such as diapers is both a waste of resources and a source of harmful pollutants. The convenience of disposal products is often of greater value than a concern for the environment. Similarly, the use of automobiles instead of public transportation systems is another example of Americans placing less value on the environment than their own convenience.

Plastics used for convenience packaging by fast-food restaurants and supermarkets are another source of pollutants. Plastics do not decompose easily and are made from valuable non-renewable petrochemical resources; however, both the businesses and consumers find it convenient to continue to use plastic products.

# Protecting the Environment

Each year, the *National Wildlife Magazine* in the United States publishes an assessment of the state of the environment based on the opinions of both its editorial staff and experts. In the 1988 review, the editors found that in most respects the quality of the environment during 1987 had not improved. Twelve new species of wildlife were added to the endangered list and the dusky seaside sparrow became extinct. During that year, there was little attempt at conservation of energy; the United States mined 897 million tonnes of coal, a record amount. Yet, the quality of air generally improved, although 60 cities found it impossible to meet the federal guidelines for clean air.

One positive sign was that in a survey of 1500 people, 91 percent said that they would be willing to pay higher taxes rather than have the government cut back on important pollution control programs. This concern by ordinary citizens is a key reason why the government continues to make and enforce regulations on environmental issues.

## Recycling and Prevention

Disposing of waste materials properly is one side of the environmental problem; preventing waste is the other. Attempts are being made to create less waste by conserving resources. Even so, the United States still produces about four billion tonnes of solid waste a year. This is about 45 kg for each person in the country every day (just a little less than the weight of an average grade 9 student).

Two methods of conservation are **recycling** and the reduction of unnecessary packaging materials. Much of the garbage produced by homes and businesses could be recycled. Typically, about one-third of garbage is paper, one-fifth is glass and metals, and about one-sixth is waste foodstuffs. Many cities are now running recycling programs where paper, metals, and glass are separated from the rest of the garbage by home-owners.

Seattle's recycling program has been one of the most successful to date. The city already recycles 28 percent of its wastes and hopes to reach 60 percent by 1994. Twenty-five hundred tonnes of bottles, cans, and newspapers are recycled each month. For every tonne of paper made from recycled fibre, Seattle residents save about 1600 kg of trees and about 100 000 L of water. Residents who separate recyclable waste are charged less for garbage collection. This is an example of how conservationists can use the forces of the marketplace to achieve their goals.

**Figure 10.8** *A Recycle America truck in Seattle's north end*

Disposable plastic packaging makes up over one-third of the plastic materials produced in the United States. Environmentalists are working at convincing business leaders and government officials that changes should be made in packaging requirements.

## PROGRESS CHECK

1. **In what ways do social and economic factors influence the amount of waste Americans create?**
2. **What are two conservation methods used to reduce the amount of waste?**
3. **In percentage terms, how much garbage in the average home is paper, glass, foodstuffs?**

# Who Protects the Environment?

Adam Smith's theory of the market economy has proven to be very successful in the United States, in that Americans enjoy a high standard of living; however, the theory of the "invisible hand" has been less successful. Rules and regulations are needed by governments to protect the public interest. Federal, state, and local governments continue to play an active role in the American market economy.

There are many examples of private industry using creative ideas and new technologies to clean up the environment. For example, a 3M company plant in Knoxville, Iowa, installed a pipe to catch solvent vapours which were then piped to the plant boilers and burned as fuel. It cost $270 000 to install this device, but the plant saved $155 000 in fuel costs in the first year. In another case, 3M began to clean reactor vessels using sonic cleaning rather than water and saved $575 000 in the first year. The cost of changing from water to sonic cleaning was only $35 000. By 1986, the 3M company had saved almost $400 million through waste-reduction measures. This is a hopeful sign that private businesses can find ways to improve the environment **and** make a profit.

These examples show that there is some truth to Adam Smith's theory that the "invisible hand" will look after the public interest in a market economy; however, these kinds of positive examples are not too common. It seems that rules and regulations are still needed by federal, state, and local governments to protect the environment.

The federal government passed its first pollution control law in 1899. In 1970, 15 separate federal pollution programs were combined to form the Environmental Protection Agency. The EPA reports directly to the president and has the power to set and enforce pollution standards, carry out research and help state and local governments with their pollution control programs. This agency carries the burden of national environmental protection.

Figure 10.9 shows that businesses have contributed the largest share of money for pollution control. Of course, it is consumers who indirectly pay these costs through higher prices. Private citizens in the United States have been directly responsible for founding some of the most influential environmental **lobby groups**, including such organizations as Ducks Unlimited, Friends of the Earth, the National Audubon Society, the National Parks Association,

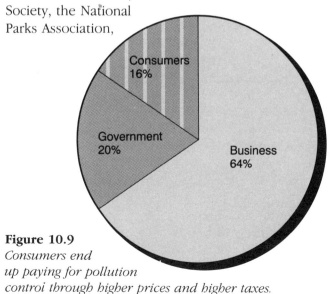

**Figure 10.9**
*Consumers end up paying for pollution control through higher prices and higher taxes.*

the Sears, Roebuck Foundation, and the Sierra Club. These lobby groups try to influence the government to make laws to protect the natural environment.

As environmental standards are raised, companies will have to develop ways to create their products without damaging the environment. In most cases, pollution controls will increase costs which consumers will help to pay. Environmental problems will only be solved, however, if industries, consumers, unions, and governments work together.

# Summary

This chapter has examined environmental problems in the United States in order to see how the public interest is served in a market economy. It is clear that there is a need for active government involvement to set rules and regulations to protect the environment. The idea of the "invisible hand" of industry naturally doing the right thing in the public interest generally does not work. What is good for business and the consumer is not necessarily good for society. Citizens expect their government to make laws for the public good. In the American market economy, the government does intervene when necessary to protect the public interest.

# Checking Back

1. The primary economic responsibility of the federal government is not to make choices for people, but to provide an environment in which people can make their own choices.

   — Ronald Reagan, *former president of the United States.*

   Based on this quotation, what do you think Reagan's attitude was toward making tough rules to protect the environment?
2. Review the different types of pollution discussed in this chapter. In point form, list the causes of each type of pollution and what is being done to prevent or reduce the pollution.

# Understanding Concepts

3. Use examples from this chapter to show how technology creates pollution problems and how it is used to solve pollution problems.
4. Locating A Toxic Waste Site: A Role-Playing Activity
   A toxic waste dump is to be located within your community. The town council has decided to create a landfill site on the edge of town. The landfill site will also handle toxic wastes produced by a local industry. Select one of the following roles, determine what your position would be on this issue, and prepare a presentation to support your point of view.
   (a) the president of the company producing the toxic wastes
   (b) a parent who works for the company and who has an asthmatic child with breathing difficulties
   (c) a citizen who wants the landfill site because it will provide jobs
   (d) an environmentalist from the local university
   (e) the mayor.

# Enrichment

5. Do any environmental lobby groups have a chapter in your community? If there are such groups, invite a representative to your class. If there is no such group in your area, write to an organization for information about their activities.
6. Predict the impact on the world if the greenhouse effect does result in a warming of the earth.
7. Ask a government official from your area to speak to the class about the role of government in protecting the environment.
8. Write a book report on Adam Smith's book, *The Wealth of Nations.*
9. Research examples of efforts by private industry or individuals to find ways of cleaning up the environment.

# CHAPTER 11

# Economic Values and the Quality of Life

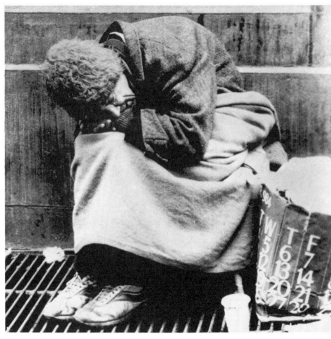

I n this chapter, basic American economic values will be examined. **Values** are things considered important to a person or group of people. Americans value such things as freedom, equality of opportunity, and national security. The Constitution guarantees "life, liberty, and the pursuit of happiness" and states that "all men are created free and equal." Sometimes, though, people are selective about applying their values. Most Americans will claim to value freedom and equality, yet many individuals and groups in the country face discrimination. An understanding of basic values provides us with some background to evaluate the **quality of life** in the United States.

American values will be examined by looking at some recent issues and trends in the United States, specifically **equality of opportunity**, **civil rights**, and **sports**. The way a nation spends money also tells us much about what is and what is not valued, so the main items of the United States **budget** will also be examined.

## FOCUS QUESTIONS

1. **How is the quality of life for people in the United States affected by economic values?**
2. **What factors determine the amount of money a person can make in the American market economy?**
3. **What does the federal budget tell us about the economic values of the American government?**

## CONCEPTS

values
quality of life
affirmative action
civil rights

social programs
budget

# Quality of Life in the United States

In 1989, the U.S.-based Marriott hotel chain had difficulty finding enough qualified workers for their new hotel in Hong Kong. They decided to improve working conditions by introducing the five-day work week common in North America. This move upset the Hong Kong business community because it threatened their traditional six-day work week. They were afraid that workers in other businesses would begin to demand a shorter work week. A five-day work week would improve the quality of life of workers in Hong Kong, but would cost businesses more for salaries, benefits, and administration expenses. Improvements in the quality of life usually cost money.

There are many factors to consider in determining the quality of life of people. Here are some indicators. Can you think of others?
- length of workday and work weeks
- amount of pay
- political, economic, and religious freedoms
- quality of food, clothing, and shelter
- opportunities for recreation and relaxation
- quality of the environment
- access to health care
- opportunities for education

As you can see from this list, some factors are economic, such as wages, hours worked, economic opportunities, and the length of the work week. Others are not economic; examples are time for relaxation, religious freedom, and a clean environment. These last three examples illustrate the fact that money alone does not ensure a high quality of life.

All people, however, must have equal economic opportunities in a market economy. This allows all who wish to work hard and take risks to improve their own quality of life. Unfortunately, in the United States, as in other countries, certain groups of people have fewer opportunities than others. We will examine three such groups in American society—working women, visible minorities, and the poor.

## Women in the Workplace

Throughout the history of the United States, there has been a great deal of discrimination against women and minority groups in many areas of the American economy. The federal government decided to protect women from discrimination by passing a series of laws. In 1964, Congress passed a Civil Rights Act which, among other things, prevented job discrimination on the basis of gender. In 1971, the United States Supreme Court ruled that unequal treatment based on gender violates the 14th Amendment to the Constitution guaranteeing all citizens equal protection under the law. In 1975, the Equal Credit Opportunity Act was passed into law. This Act makes it illegal for financial institutions such as banks to discriminate against customers on the basis of sex or marital status.

On the other hand, the fight for women's rights received a setback when the **Equal Rights Amendment (ERA)** to the Constitution failed to pass into law. This proposed amendment stated: "Equality of rights under the law shall not be denied or abridged by the United States or any state on account of sex." The amendment was first introduced into Congress in 1923 by the National Women's Party; however, it was not passed by the House of Representatives until 1971, almost 50 years later! The Senate passed it in 1972, but to become binding on all the states, it had to be passed by 38 of the 50 state legislatures (three-quarters of the total number). By the deadline of June 30, 1982, only 35 states had ratified the amendment, so it did not become law.

**Figure 11.1** *A hard-fought campaign to ratify the Equal Rights Amendment to the Constitution failed, but progress has been made on many women's issues.*

In spite of some progress in recent years, women have tended to remain in low-paying jobs—clerical work, retail sales, and the like. These types of jobs have been referred to as the "pink-collar ghetto" (as opposed to blue-collar manual labour jobs and white-collar managerial and professional jobs). In order to correct these inequalities, municipal, state, and federal governments have begun **affirmative action** programs. The goal of these programs is to increase the number of women and members of minority groups in the work force. Wherever the numbers are too low, employers must make positive efforts to hire members of these groups. Critics argue that affirmative action programs simply discriminate in reverse. These critics claim you should not use discrimination to fight discrimination.

Table 11.1 shows that the number of women in the working population has changed during the course of this century. Table 11.2 shows that there has been some shift of women into managerial and professional positions during the 1980s.

**Table 11.1** *Women in the Working Population*

| YEAR | WORKING WOMEN AS PERCENT OF FEMALE POPULATION* | WORKING WOMEN AS PERCENT OF TOTAL POPULATION* |
|---|---|---|
| 1900 | 18.8 | 18.3 |
| 1910 | 21.5 | 19.9 |
| 1920 | 21.4 | 20.4 |
| 1930 | 22.0 | 22.0 |
| 1940 | 25.4 | 24.3 |
| 1950 | 33.9 | 29.0 |
| 1960 | 37.8 | 32.5 |
| 1970 | 43.4 | 37.2 |
| 1980 | 51.6 | 42.0 |
| 1987 | 56.1 | 44.3 |

*Aged 10 years and over

**Table 11.2** *Occupations of Employed Women (percentages)*

| OCCUPATIONS | 1981 | 1987 |
|---|---|---|
| Managerial & professional | 20.9 | 24.4 |
| Technical sales & administrative support | 45.9 | 45.1 |
| Service occupations | 18.8 | 18.1 |
| Precision production, craft, repair | 1.9 | 2.3 |
| Operators, fabricators, labourers | 11.1 | 9.0 |
| Farming, forestry, fishing | 1.3 | 1.1 |

## PROGRESS CHECK

1. **List five factors that affect people's quality of life.**
2. **What was the purpose of the Equal Credit Opportunity Act?**
3. **Why did the ERA amendment fail to become law?**
4. **What is meant by "affirmative action" programs?**

## Civil Rights

One of the most important social changes to occur in the United States in the 1960s was the civil rights movement. The goal of this movement was to ensure that blacks and other visible minorities have full equality with whites. One of the high points of the movement occurred on August 28, 1963, when 200 000 people converged on Washington, DC, in a protest march.

Despite the assassinations of President John F. Kennedy, Senator **Robert Kennedy**, and the civil rights leader **Martin Luther King Jr.**, the movement made significant gains with the passage of two major pieces of legislation under President **Lyndon Johnson**. The first of these, the Civil Rights Act of 1964, was the most significant civil rights legislation in American history. Besides providing protection for women, it also required businesses that serve the public to do so without regard to race, colour, religion, or national origin. Discrimination in the workplace was made illegal, and an Equal Employment Opportunity Commission was established. Federal funds were to be cut off from any program or activity which showed evidence of racial discrimination.

The Civil Rights Act of 1968 sought to end discrimination in the sale and rental of housing. This Act was supported by a Supreme Court decision in the same year. In fact, the Court's decision confirmed a law that had been in place since 1866. Laws alone are not enough to protect people from discrimination if these laws are not enforced.

## The Poor

In the early 1980s, there were about 35 million Americans living below the **poverty line**. This was about 14 percent of the total population. The poverty line can be set at any level. The American government has decided that people are below the poverty line when they must spend more than one-third of their income for food. If a person has an income of $900 per month but requires more than $300 to feed a family, that person would be below the poverty line. The number of poor in the United States increased during the early 1980s, even though the American economy was growing rapidly. The gap between the incomes of the poor and the rest of the population has widened since 1960.

Poverty in America is more common among women, the young, the old, and in the non-white population. These are the groups in society that collectively have the least power. In the past, women were denied equal access to education, and so had little economic power. In addition, attitudes in some parts of society discourage women from taking active roles outside the home, giving them little opportunity to acquire social or political power.

Visible minorities have had a long history of discrimination in the United States. In spite of new laws in the past few decades, attitudes are changing slowly. Blacks, Spanish-Americans, and Asian-Americans still find themselves struggling to get economic equality with "mainstream" Americans. Visible minorities are overrepresented in low-paying jobs and underrepresented in managerial and professional positions.

Governments and social institutions have attempted to deal with the problems of poverty in many ways. Unemployment insurance supports workers for short periods between jobs; social assistance provides for basic needs for people unable to work. Educational programs and job retraining plans have been set up to help people get the skills they need to get jobs that pay well. Food banks, subsidized housing, free clinics, crisis centres, and soup kitchens have all played a role in helping the poor.

But the one inescapable fact is that, for the poor, the quality of life declined in the 1980s. Many critics point to the cuts in government spending on social programs as an important cause of this. One civil rights leader claimed that the real legacy of President Reagan's administration of the 1980s is 35 million poor people.

**Figure 11.2** *The poverty line can be set at different levels.*

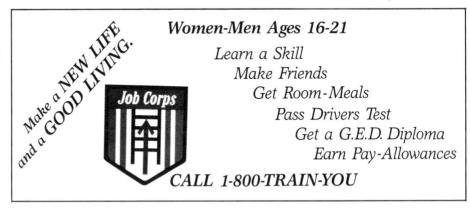

**Figure 11.3** *Programs have been set up to provide people with opportunities to improve their quality of life through employment.*

## PROGRESS CHECK

1. **How is the poverty line determined?**
2. **Which groups in society are more prone to poverty? Why?**

# Sports in American Society

Sports are an important part of the economy of the United States and illustrate some basic economic values held by Americans. Sports are part of the massive entertainment industry, which includes television, motion pictures, recording artists, musicians, and amusement parks.

In 1976, the American writer, **James Michener**, wrote a book called *Sports in America*. Michener claimed that the United States, as a country, placed just about the right emphasis on sports. His ranking of 16 countries according to how much emphasis they place on sports is shown in Table 11.3.

**Table 11.3** *Comparison of the Emphasis on Sports in 16 Selected Nations*

| EXCESSIVE EMPHASIS | WELL ABOVE AVERAGE EMPHASIS | ABOUT RIGHT EMPHASIS | WELL BELOW AVERAGE EMPHASIS |
|---|---|---|---|
| East Germany | Japan | Britain | Mexico |
| USSR | Australia | United States | Ireland |
| South Africa | Italy | Belgium | Sweden |
| Brazil | Hungary | Spain | India |

Measuring how much emphasis is placed on sports in a country is very difficult. In many communist countries, the government directly subsidizes sports. These countries place a high value on achievement in international competitions like the Olympics. Money is made available to produce super athletes. This is one reason why communist countries usually win many Olympic medals.

In the United States, the sports industry operates mainly within the rules of a free market economy. This means that amateur athletes cannot rely on government funds for support; however, many businesses sponsor sporting events and athletes for advertising purposes. The businesses use the athletic events to promote their products while the athletes get the money they need for training facilities and competitions.

Professional athletes in the United States are much like entrepreneurs. They have a particular skill that they sell to the highest bidder. Team owners buy their services in order to make a winning team to draw more fans to watch the sport. They are in the business to make money, much of which comes through ticket sales. An outstanding athlete can make enormous amounts of money because of the fans that person attracts to the sporting events. The fans (consumers) end up paying the salaries to athletes and profits to owners.

In 1988, **Wayne Gretzky** was traded from the Edmonton Oilers hockey team to the Los Angeles Kings. The owner of the Los Angeles Kings paid $15 million just to buy Gretzky's contract. The

**Figure 11.4** *Wayne Gretzky in 1989. How is the economic value of a hockey player determined?*

services of professional athletes are "owned" and can be "sold" or traded by owners. The value of a player is set by the market; the better the player, the higher the demand from other teams, and the higher the salary the player can earn. In some sports, the best athletes can get millions of dollars while those at the bottom may be lucky to earn a minimum wage.

Was the Gretzky deal a good investment? **Bruce McNall**, the Los Angeles team owner, claims that his investment will be paid off within two years. The team sold over 4000 more season tickets and sold out more games in the 1988-89 season than ever before. That year, the Kings made the playoffs; each home game was worth about $500 000 in income. Ticket and advertising sales earned the Kings about $10 million dollars in the first year alone. The fans/consumers in Los Angeles voted "yes" with their money!

The popularity of a sport depends on fan interest. In the United States, the most popular professional sport is baseball, followed by football, basketball, and hockey. Baseball players, as a group, make the most money. In 1988, the

*average* salary of major league baseball players was $438 729. The "marketplace" is cited as the reason for this high figure. Teams know that if they do not offer good salaries to good players, other teams will. The popularity of baseball allows teams to pay huge salaries and still make profits.

Major league franchises are important to the economies of cities in which they are located. One study carried out in the mid-1970s found that the Pittsburgh Pirates baseball team brought $21 million into the economy of Pittsburgh each year. Pirates' games attracted over 500 000 people from outside the city.

**Table 11.4** *Average Salary for Baseball Players in Selected Teams*

| TEAM | AVERAGE SALARIES | RANK |
|---|---|---|
| New York Yankees | $718 670 | 1 |
| Detroit Tigers | $612 326 | 2 |
| Boston Red Sox | $610 170 | 3 |
| New York Mets | $605 895 | 4 |
| Los Angeles Dodgers | $573 441 | 5 |
| Toronto Blue Jays | $484 427 | 10 |
| Montreal Expos | $343 047 | 20 |
| Chicago White Sox | $226 389 | 26 |

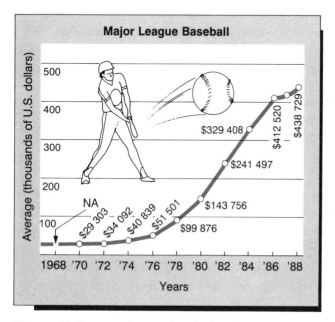

**Figure 11.5** *Major league baseball salaries, 1970–1988*

**Figure 11.6** *Skilled professional athletes make very high salaries, but often generate good revenues for their owners.*

A study of the 1989 Super Bowl in Miami estimated that this one football game generated $1.9 *billion* in revenues nation-wide. This was the biggest one-day, money-making sports event in history. Much of the money was generated in an indirect manner. For example, it was estimated that 25 million Americans across the country attended Super Bowl parties. At an average cost of $30 per person, this alone would generate $750 million. The city of Miami collected $100 000 in parking fees and another $144 million from visitors who came to southern Florida for the game. The NBC television network paid $18 million for the broadcast rights. The NFL paid $4.8 million to the winning and losing teams. On top of all this, it was estimated that an additional $2.5 billion was spent around the world on betting. Up to 30 million Americans (about one in every eight) placed some kind of bet on the game.

It has been estimated that the United States sporting industry is worth at least $50 billion a year, making it a very important industry.

How do salaries of professional athletes compare with other occupations? Table 11.5 lists a number of occupations along with their average annual salaries. In theory, workers' salaries are determined by supply and demand. The more workers there are available, the lower the wages; the harder skilled workers are to find, the higher the salary. In a market economy, however, salaries can be set for non-economic reasons. For example, some professions, such as doctors and lawyers, control the number (supply) of new graduates entering the profession. By controlling the supply, salaries can be kept high; thus, the average salary for neurosurgeons is $203 570 while an elementary school teacher's salary is $24 762. Also, collective action by workers can force employers to pay higher wages than supply and demand would suggest. And, there are traditions that affect the economy. In the past, men have been paid more for doing much the same work as women. As these traditions change, the market economy of the United States will also change.

**Table 11.5** *Average Salaries of Selected Groups*

| OCCUPATION | SALARY RANGE |
|---|---|
| Accountants | $20 000–50 000 |
| Attorneys | $35 000–65 000 |
| Clerks | $8000–20 000 |
| Engineers | $25 000–80 000 |
| Nursing Assistants | $8000–18 000 |
| Registered Nurses | $18 000–35 000 |
| Secretaries | $13 000–30 000 |
| Typists | $11 000–17 000 |

**PROGRESS CHECK**

1. **Where does the United States rank in terms of emphasis on sports?**
2. **Explain why baseball players are able to earn very high salaries.**
3. **Identify several direct and indirect ways that a Super Bowl game stimulates the economy.**
4. **Salaries are not always set on the basis of supply and demand. Write a paragraph explaining this statement.**

# American Values and the Federal Budget Process

The values which Americans hold as a group are reflected in the federal budget. Figure 11.7 shows federal spending for 1987. Although the **Entitlement programs**, which provide services to the needy, represent the largest share of this budget, it is worth noting that defence spending in the United States consumes almost 30 percent of the total budget. This is much higher than the percentage allocated by other countries, such as Canada, which spends less than 10 percent of the federal budget on defence.

**$284.9**
**National defence**

Military salaries
Military and family housing
Weapons, planes, ships, tanks, trucks
Research and development programs
Intelligence operations
General operations and maintenance

**$102.3**
**Non-defence discretionary spending**

General government operations, including salaries, benefits, and administrative costs
International affairs and foreign aid
Space program
Medical research
National parks
Conservation programs
Student loans
Interstate highway system

**$455.8**
**Entitlement programs**

Social security
Medicare
Medicaid
Aid to families with dependent children
Food stamps
Public housing
Unemployment compensation
Food and nutrition assistance
Low-income home energy assistance
Civilian and military retirement

**$148.0**
**Interest on the national debt**

*all figures in billions

**Figure 11.7** *The United States federal budget for 1987*

The United States and the Soviet Union are the world's biggest military spenders. Not everyone agrees that this should be the case. A pro-peace book called *World Military And Social Expenditures 1985*, tries to put military expenditures into perspective.

- Governments on a worldwide basis spent an average of $26 600 per soldier, but only $450 per student.
- For every $11 spent on medical research, $45 was spent on military research.
- There is one soldier for every 43 people in the world, but only one physician for every 1030 people.
- The amount spent on international peacekeeping was only 6 cents for every person in the world compared to $152 for military expenditures.
- The budget of the United States Air Force is larger than the total educational budgets for 1.2 billion children in Africa, Latin America, and Asia (excluding Japan).
- The total military budget of the Soviet Union is larger than all the money spent on education for 3.6 billion people in the developing countries.

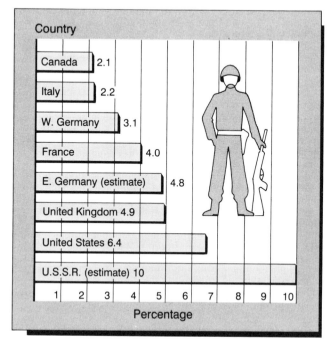

**Figure 11.8** *The United States spends more on defence than most other countries.*

In the United States, choices between social programs and military spending are made during the budget debates. Figure 11.9 shows how the budget is decided on. During the summer-fall period, the various federal agencies give reasons to justify their budget requests. They try to show how their programs are important to the nation and will benefit Americans. During the winter months, the various agencies and departments present their cases to Congress through public hearings, written reports, and by lobbying members of Congress. In Washington, there are about 10 000 people who are full-time lobbyists representing different interest groups. These interest groups include such organizations as:

- the Vietnam Veterans of America, who try to increase medical benefits for veterans of the Vietnam War;
- the American Association of Retired Persons, which tries to improve social security and Medicare benefits for those retired;
- the National Farmers Organization, a group defending farm subsidy programs;
- the Sierra Club, promoting environmental protection;
- the American Federation of Government Employees, an association to protect the interests of civil servants; and
- the National Taxpayers Union, whose members seek to reduce taxes.

Lobby groups try to get legislation passed which favours their interests. The National Rifle Association of America (NRA), for example, has some three million members (including President **George Bush**) and lobbies against the passage of any gun control legislation.

When all the interested groups have had their say, the federal government sets the budget. The money each federal agency gets is a reflection of the values of the government leaders. The major struggles for more money are usually between supporters of military and social programs. Republican presidents such as **Richard Nixon**, Ronald Reagan, and George Bush tended toward more military spending, while Democratic presidents like John F. Kennedy, Lyndon Johnson, and **Jimmy Carter** favoured social programs. Regardless of politics, though, military spending in the United States has remained high throughout the years.

**The Federal Budget Process**

**Spring**
Office of Management and Budget (OMB) assigns government agencies a maximum amount for their budget proposals.

**Summer-Fall**
Agencies submit their proposed budgets to OMB. Agency directors meet with OMB executives and the president's staff to justify proposed spending and to finalize the budget.

**January**
The president submits his budget proposal to Congress.

**February**
Congressional committees submit program estimates to budget committees.

**April**
Budget committees report the first budget resolution. The resolution sets targets for government spending by Congress.

**May**
Congress completes action on first budget resolution. Neither house may consider authorization or spending bills, or changes in tax revenues or the national debt until the first budget resolution is adopted.

**May-August**
Congress completes action on all budget and spending bills.

**September**
Congress completes action on a reconciliation bill to bring the budget in line with spending bills. Congress may not adjourn until it completes action on these measures.

**October 1**
Fiscal year begins

**Figure 11.9** *The federal budget process*

133

## PROGRESS CHECK

1. **What was the dollar value of the two largest categories in the 1987 federal budget?**
2. **Which countries are the biggest military spenders? Suggest reasons why each would spend so much money on military programs.**
3. **List three lobby groups that try to influence the budget, and identify their main concerns.**

### AN ISSUE: THE RIGHT TO OWN GUNS

The right to own guns is an issue that points out the different values held in Canada and the United States. In the United States, the NRA has been successful in fighting against gun controls in spite of mounting evidence against their position. In 1987, there were 20 000 murders in the United States, with guns used in 12 000. Canada had 642 murders, 200 of which were committed with guns.

The cities of Seattle in Washington State, and Vancouver, British Columbia, are very similar in terms of location and population; however, the murder rate in Seattle is five times higher than in Vancouver. These statistics are even more significant considering that Seattle has a *lower* than normal rate of murders for American cities while Vancouver has a *higher* than normal rate for Canadian cities. Detroit, Chicago, New York, Houston, and Los Angeles all have much higher murder rates than Seattle. Washington, D.C., the nation's capital, has the worst murder rate.

The NRA dismissed the study that pointed out the Seattle-Vancouver differences as "an insult to the intelligence." They argued that Americans have the constitutional right to own guns and no government should tamper with that right. The availability of guns has made life in many American cities much more dangerous than in typical Canadian cities. This has a negative effect on the quality of life in the United States.

The noted American sociologist and political scientist, **Seymour Lipset**, states that " . . . while Canadians and Americans share many of the same values, Canadians are on the whole more conservative, law-abiding, collectively oriented, and less driven by the desire to achieve than are Americans."

**Figure 11.10** *Brochures from the National Rifle Association promoting their point of view*

# Summary

This chapter took a brief look at some American values and issues about the quality of life. Questions were raised about equality of opportunity and civil rights in the United States and the effect of the market economy in creating poverty. The value of sports in the economy was also considered. The chapter concluded with a look at the American budget and budget process. The emphasis placed on military spending in the budget illustrates the value of national security to Americans.

# Checking Back

1. What are some of the key economic values in the United States? How are these values reflected in the federal budget and in the salaries paid to professional athletes?
2. Write a short paper discussing why women, visible minorities, and the poor have less economic power than mainstream Americans.

# Understanding Concepts

3. Briefly describe the salaries of major league baseball players. Using the concepts of market economy and supply and demand, explain why these salaries are so high.
4. Nothing is more characteristic of Canadians than the inclination to be moderate.
   —**Vincent Massey**, On Being Canadian, 1948.

   What do you think Massey meant by this statement? Write two similar statements, one to describe Canadians and the other to describe Americans.

# Enrichment

5. Does money buy happiness? Explain your decision.
6. Issue: Should the United States spend more money on social programs and less on defence?
   Use the information comparing military spending and social programs, write a position paper on this topic. Use your library for any additional material you might need.
7. Seymour Lipset claims that important differences between Americans and Canadians began to emerge during the American Revolution of 1776. While many American colonists fought for the revolution, many others chose to remain loyal to Britain. Those who escaped to Canada became known as the Loyalists. Lipset states that these Loyalists

   > . . . built a society in which there was deference to law and authority, a large role for government, and close relations between the established churches and the state. In contrast, the United States was formed in the cauldron of revolution, and its founding principles included a strong faith in individual rights and achievement, a profound suspicion of government, and the separation of church and state. These differences still persist despite the passage of time. They are the core values of two distinct societies.
   > (Source: Eli Mandel and David Taras, eds. *A Passion for Canadian Identity: An Introduction to Canadian Studies*)

   (a) What hypothesis does Lipset pose to explain the differences between the two nations?
   (b) What supporting evidence does he give?
   (c) Do you agree with his argument?
   (d) If possible, find out about the views of other writers who take entirely different positions on this question.

# CHAPTER 12

# *Looking into the Future*

**W**ill the United States remain a leading industrial power in the 21st century? How will the United States deal with change? In this chapter, the changing patterns of American economic activity will be discussed, as will some predictions about the future of the American economy. The impact of changes on the global economy and trade patterns will also be examined.

## FOCUS QUESTIONS

1. What changes will affect the market economy in the United States?
2. What effect might the changing global economy and trade patterns have on the United States?

## CONCEPTS

| | | |
|---|---|---|
| change | protectionism | free trade |
| robotics | tariffs | |

# The Need to Predict Change

Americans must deal with many issues in the future. For example, humankind now faces enormous global environmental problems, such as acid rain, the greenhouse effect, and depletion of the ozone layer. The major industrial economies of the world, including the United States, created these problems and now must find solutions to them. The world's economy must deal with other challenges, such as underdevelopment in poor nations, international debt, the shift of power to the Pacific Rim, and the development of new trade blocs. What responsibility will the United States take in dealing with these problems? How will the American market economy respond to the changing world of the future? These are questions that American government, labour, and business leaders are facing.

Predicting change accurately is important for any business in a market economy. Predicting the correct trends can mean the difference between success or failure. Many companies hire planners to foresee the future. For example, computer companies want to know if the home computer market will grow or decline. Remember that Apple computers were built for this untapped market that had been ignored by the computer companies. Will people continue to be interested in fast-food restaurants? McDonald's will certainly be interested in predicting this trend.

**John Naisbitt** is an American writer whose book, *Megatrends*, predicts a number of trends emerging in the United States:

- the aging of the American population;
- the **privatization** of government services;
- the importance of family related issues such as day-care;
- increasing concern for the environment;
- continuing education for adults who wish to retrain; and
- a highly sophisticated consumer market.

If these predictions are accurate, they will have a strong influence on the American economy. For example, the article "Angry consumers boycotting Exxon" illustrates the increased awareness of consumers and their concern for the

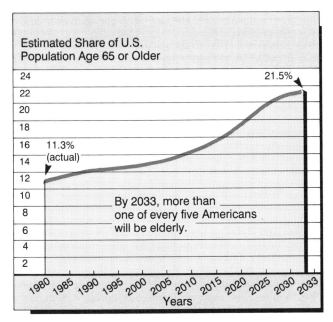

**Figure 12.1** *Growth in the number of elderly Americans*

# Angry consumers boycotting Exxon

**By Marilyn Kalfus**
(Orange County Register)

Gordon Penge protested at San Clemente Exxon with a handmade sign. Rob Orth ripped up his Exxon credit card and mailed it back to the company. Art Kassel, a private investigator who each week fills his Oldsmobile with about $100 in gasoline, is taking his business elsewhere.

lic are focused on the price of gasoline, the highest since February, 1986.

But some people, such as James Yogurtian of Fountain Valley, Calif., are even more outraged over the environmental damage.

Oran⸻ are⸻

**Figure 12.2** *Consumers are becoming concerned about the environment, so businesses will have to adjust their practices or face the consequences.*

environment. If this trend continues, businesses will have to be more careful about the environment. Because of this, jobs will be lost in some industries, but created in others. Entrepreneurs will emerge to develop new technologies to help clean the environment.

Dealing with change is difficult. Throughout history, people have resisted large-scale change. For instance, in the early days of the United States, many people opposed replacing canals with railroads. An irate citizen wrote this letter to President Andrew Jackson in 1828.

---

*Dear Mr. President.*

*The canal system of this country is being threatened by the spread of a new form of transportation known as railroads. The federal government must preserve the canals.*

*As you well know, Mr. President, railroad carriages are pulled at the enormous speed of 15 miles per hour. The Almighty certainly never intended that people should move at such breakneck speed.*

*Signed*
*Martin Van Buren*

---

**Figure 12.3**

This letter was not written by a foolish crank. **Martin van Buren** was the governor of New York State and went on to become the eighth president of the United States!

# Changing Economic Patterns in the United States

One important change in the American economy is the decline of the manufacturing sector and the rise of the service sector. Figure 12.4 shows just how quickly the service sector has grown since the end of World War II. A number of factors have contributed to this trend, but one of the most important is the increased affluence of the American people.

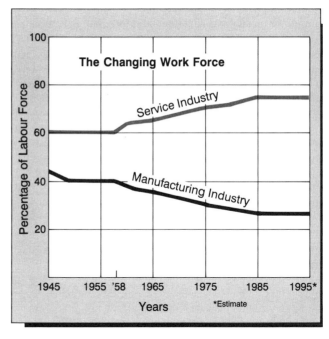

**Figure 12.4** *Suggest several reasons for the trends shown in this graph concerning the American labour force.*

Another trend has been the movement of people to the South and West of the country. During the 1970s, almost three-quarters of all new jobs were created in the Sun Belt. These changes

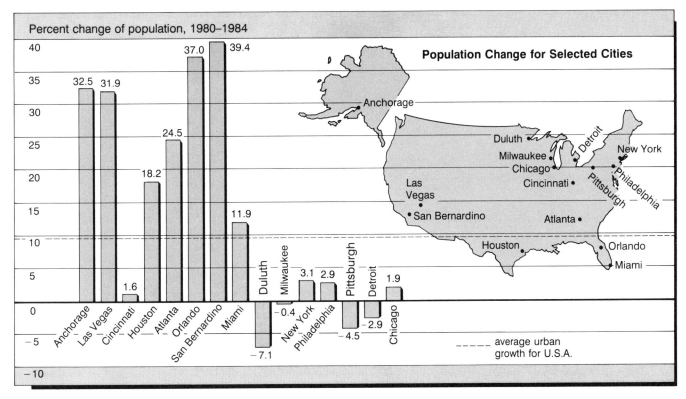

**Figure 12.5** *This graph shows growth rates for some cities. In which parts of the country are cities growing the fastest?*

have continued into the 1980s. By the year 2000, it is estimated that one in five Americans — over 50 million people — will live in the states of California, Texas, and Florida. Businesses will have to adjust to this shift in the location of their markets.

Another major change that will affect the American economy is the introduction of **robotics**. Figure 12.6 shows that the period 1985–1990 was a takeoff period for the use of robots in the United States. Robot use will continue, with these machines doing more work in American factories and businesses. Government, labour, and business will all feel the economic impact of robots.

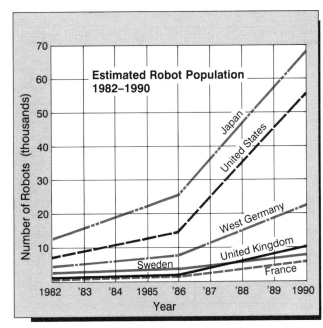

**Figure 12.6** *Robot populations will grow in most industrialized countries.*

The **Hudson Institute** is an American "think tank" that tries to predict the future. In 1983, it predicted a rapid increase in these technologies:

- inexhaustible and/or inexpensive energy sources;
- "pollution-free" industries;
- telecommunications;
- bioengineering;
- space travel and manufacturing;
- robots and automation; and
- computers.

The Hudson Institute is already correct in its predictions about new technologies in bioengineering, telecommunications, robots, and computers. Research into **cold fusion** could lead to an "inexhaustible energy", and manufacturing in space is in the planning stages. As these technologies develop, there will be adjustments in the market economy.

**Figure 12.7**

## PROGRESS CHECK

1. **Why is it important for a business to predict future trends?**
2. **According to Figure 12.4, what percentage of the work force is now in the manufacturing sector? service industries?**
3. **Which cities grew by over 20 percent between 1980 and 1984? Which cities lost population during this period?**
4. **What is meant by the term "Sun Belt"? Suggest reasons why this area is a desirable place to live.**
5. **Select one prediction listed by the Hudson Institute and give examples to show that the prediction is true.**

## Global Markets and Trade

The United States is both the largest exporting and the largest importing nation in the world. It will continue to be the world's largest economy into the next century.

---

**READ FOR INFORMATION**

**1. The Source**
This article was written by a reporter for American Press (AP) in Tokyo, Japan. It was found in the *Calgary Herald* on February 16, 1989.

**2. Main Idea**
The heading and these paragraphs tell us that the predicted technology is a tiny medical robot that could be used in patients.

# Tiny robot under way

TOKYO (AP) — Japanese scientists have begun developing a tiny robot to move inside the human body to treat diseased tissue, a professor said Wednesday.

The scientists eventually hope to produce a robot that can transmit its location and findings, and can cut or otherwise treat diseased parts, said Iwao Fujimasa of Tokyo University's Research Centre for Advanced Science and Technology.

"Researchers for many years have sent probes to study the oceans and outer space; we hope to be able to study the inner world."

Fujimasa, an artificial-heart specialist, said the goal is a robot less than 0.10 cm in size that will be able to travel through veins and inside organs.

The project will require that the smallest currently available parts, such as motors, gears, and screws, be reduced to about one-thousandth their present size. Even with a robot that size, the team will need to study how to minimize problems created by its presence in the body, such as blocking blood flow.

Since September, the group has received financial support from the Ministry of International Trade and Industry, Fujimasa said. It hopes the ministry will agree to fund an International Micromachine Centre costing the equivalent of about $100 million Cdn and provide annual funding of $2 million Cdn, he said.

**3. Supporting Detail**
This gives us more information about the nature of this kind of robot.

One out of every eight American jobs is based on the export market. An estimate by the Department of Commerce in 1989 was that 25 000 jobs are created for every $1 billion in exports. That is why there was great concern during the 1980s when export sales of U.S. products fell. The reduction was mainly due to increased competition in traditional American markets from Asian countries, such as Japan, China, South Korea, and Thailand. These countries were able to produce quality products at lower prices than the United States, largely because of lower wage rates and greater productivity. Loss of worldwide sales meant fewer jobs in the United States. It has been estimated that over 2.5 million jobs have been lost to foreign competition in recent years.

The United States economy will continue to decline if improvements in production methods are not made. Many factories and plants are no longer efficient compared to other countries. In 1982, less than one-third of American steel was produced by the latest, most-efficient **continuous casting method**, whereas in Japan, about four-fifths was produced in this way.

Some critics have argued that strong government intervention in their economies has helped other countries become successful. In Japan, for example, the government has used programs that give industries a boost, such as government-sponsored research and development. Other critics suggest that it has been other countries' **protectionist** policies to their economies that has been responsible for the United States trade difficulties. Many countries have trade **tariffs** (taxes) on imported goods. Tariffs make imported goods more expensive than those made in the country. This helps local industries get established, but reduces markets for foreign products.

By contrast, the United States has tried to reduce tariffs and other **trade barriers** and to create freer trade among nations. In 1988, the United States concluded an historic free trade agreement with its biggest trading partner, Canada. After a bitter political debate in Canada, the free trade agreement went into effect on January 1, 1989.

Some economists believe that several large free-trading zones will emerge around the world, one in North America, the second in Europe, and the third centred around Japan and other Pacific Rim countries in Asia.

## PROGRESS CHECK

1. **In the United States, how many jobs are created for each billion dollars worth of exports?**
2. **What is a tariff? How do tariffs protect industries within a country?**

# Summary

This book has examined the way the United States market economy developed and how the economy meets the needs of people. During the Industrial Revolution, people like Sam Slater were dissatisfied with conditions in England and fled to the United States, bringing their new industrial knowledge with them. Entrepreneurs took these new ideas and established successful businesses. The new inventions changed the way people worked and lived; the place of work moved from cottages to factories. The factory system resulted in the growth of large cities.

Successful entrepreneurs developed huge businesses employing thousands of workers. A labour movement grew as workers organized to demand better wages and working conditions. Governments gradually reacted to public pressure and made laws to protect workers and consumers. Workers generally now have pension plans, paid holidays and vacations, and health benefits.

The pattern of American industry has been strongly affected by the geography of the country. The physical geography of the United States—the geology and soils, rainfall, temperatures, and vegetation—had a major influence on the location of primary industries. The human geography, especially the distribution of population and the historical patterns of migration, affected the growth of both manufacturing and service industries.

The role of both the entrepreneur and the consumer within the United States market economy was examined. Consumers in a market economy collectively make decisions. Businesses that meet the consumers' needs are successful; others soon disappear. Entrepreneurs are people who do a good job of recognizing the market potential that exists in society.

In the final section in this book, some basic economic values were examined. American attitudes toward protection of the environment, social programs, military spending, and the role of sports tell us much about economic values and the nature of American society.

Finally, there was an attempt to look into the future. Those businesses that adjust to changes in the economy will be able to take advantage of opportunities and challenges. The American market economy developed in response to many challenges in the past and no doubt will continue to do so in the future.

# Checking Back

1. Write a paper on the future of the American market economy. In your paper, select several trends you think will develop and describe what impact these might have on the economy.
2. Select 20 items from your home or school and determine where they were made. Categorize these according to country of origin. Which countries make the most products? What conclusions can you draw from your findings?

# Understanding Concepts

3. Compare the lives of people in the past with your prediction about the future. Use a chart like the one that follows. An example has been done for you.

| ITEM | 100 YEARS AGO | TODAY | 100 YEARS IN THE FUTURE |
|---|---|---|---|
| Long-distance communication | mostly letters | telephone, satellite | laser, fibre optics, video phones |
| Transportation | | | |
| Medicine | | | |
| Foods | | | |
| Music | | | |

*SAMPLE ONLY*

# Enrichment

4. What do you think will be the biggest-selling product in the year 2000? Give reasons for your answer.
5. Describe the impact on the economy of the United States if one of these inventions occurred:
   (a) an engine that uses water for fuel
   (b) a computer chip brain implant that gives people all the knowledge they need
   (c) medical technology to raise the life expectancy of people to 150 years
   (d) an invention of your own creation.
6. Research free trade agreements in the world. Are these agreements successful? What are the advantages and disadvantages of the free trade agreement between Canada and the United States?

# Glossary

**acid rain** — rain, snow, or other precipitation that has been polluted by acids of sulphur and nitrogen

**affirmative action** — a policy designed to correct discrimination by giving preference to minority groups who have been discriminated against in the past. A business might be required to hire a certain percentage of their workers from minority groups.

**Agricultural Revolution** — a period about 10 000 years ago when people in the Middle East began to meet their basic needs by domesticating plants and animals rather than by hunting and gathering methods

**alluvial soil** — soil that has been deposited as a result of river action

**American War of Independence** (1776-1783) — a war fought between the American colonies and Britain. It ended with the Treaty of Paris in 1783, when the colonies were granted independence.

**annexation** — to take over or occupy an area of land and make it part of your own country

**anoxic water** — water with little or no oxygen

**approval** — one of the four characteristics used to describe an institution. Each institution must be accepted by and have the approval of the population in general.

**assets** — property and capital which a business owns and which may be applied against outstanding debts

**automation** — the use of machinery, especially robots and computers, to reduce the need for human labour

**boom and bust** — a cycle of economic expansion (boom) followed by sudden collapse (bust)

**broadcasting** — a method of planting seeds which involves scattering them by hand

**budget** — a financial plan showing expected income and expenditures over a period of time

**capital** — the money which is used to finance a business venture

**cast iron** — a brittle form of iron made by pouring the molten metal into moulds

**centrally planned economy** — an economic system in which decision making is controlled by government planners

**civil rights** — the rights of a citizen of a country

**Civil Rights Act** — passed in 1968, this act sought to end discrimination based on race, colour, religion or national origin

**Clean Water Act** — passed in 1972, this act established water pollution standards

**cold fusion** — combining of two nuclei under normal temperatures to create a nucleus of greater mass, which results in a huge release of energy

**collateral** — items of value that are used to secure a loan. If the loan is not paid back, these items become the property of the lender.

**collective bargaining** — negotiations by a union or association of employees to establish a contract with an employer. This contract usually deals with pay scales and working conditions.

**commission** — pay based on a percentage of sales

**conglomerate** — a single company which owns a number of distinct subsidiary businesses

**consumer sovereignty** — the decision of consumers to buy or not to buy determines which products or services survive in the marketplace

**consumerism** — a movement started in the 1960s that tried to harness consumer power to fight against shoddy products and services

**consumers** — all people who buy goods or services

**continental divide** — in the United States, this is the line running through the Rocky Mountains. Rivers west of the divide flow to the Pacific Ocean while those to the east flow to the Atlantic Ocean.

**continuous casting method** — the latest, most efficient method of producinig steel, in which steel goes from a molten form to slabs without going through an ingot stage

**contract** — a legal agreement between two parties

**coolies** — Chinese labourers who were brought into the United States to help build the first transcontinental railroads

**corporation** — a type of business organization that can own property and make contracts

**cottage industry** — a method of industrial organization which was used before the Industrial Revolution. Work was carried on in the home or cottage of the worker rather than in a factory.

**cradle of American industry** — the name given to Sam Slater's textile mill in Pawtucket, Rhode Island

**demand** — a measure of how much consumers want a product or service

**demand line** — a line on a chart showing how demand for a product will change as price changes

**direct sales** — sales that are made in people's homes rather than commercial outlets

**distribution of population** — the way in which people are spread throughout a country

**diversified** — a diversified economy is one that has a number of important economic activities and, therefore, does not rely on a single industry, making it less susceptible to boom and bust cycles

**division of labour** — the division of manufacturing activities into a number of small steps. This was an important step in the development of mass production techniques.

**domesticating** — taming wild animals for livestock farming and cultivating wild plants for agriculture

**durable goods** — goods which are not consumed directly, such as refrigerators and automobiles

**duty** — a toll or tax charged by a government on goods which are imported or exported

**efficiency** — the ability to produce goods and services without wasted time or resources. This is one of the strengths traditionally attributed to the market economy.

**Enclosure Acts** — a series of Acts of Parliament passed over a number of centuries in Britain. They were designed to consolidate farmlands in order to increase the size of fields and improve the efficiency of farming.

**Entitlement programs** — federal programs that provide social services to the needy

**entrepreneur** — a person willing to take business risks in order to make a profit

**Environmental Protection Agency (EPA)** — an independent agency established by the federal government to enforce the protection of the environment

**Equal Rights Amendment (ERA)** — a proposed act that attempted to guarantee equal rights for women. The act was passed by Congress in 1971 but failed to get the necessary ratification by two-thirds of the

state legislatures to become an amendment to the constitution.

**equality of opportunity** — the right of all people to participate in the economic life of a country without discrimination

**equilibrium price** — the point at which the supply and demand lines of a good or service intersect

**executive branch** — a branch of the federal government made up of the president and appointed staff

**factors of production** — the resources of land, labour, and capital

**factory system** — a method of production where employees come to a central location to work

**foreign subsidiary** — a firm which is owned by a parent company located in another country

**franchise** — the right to sell a product or service, sold by the owner to someone for a fee

**free trade** — the absence of trade barriers between countries

**geographical inertia** — the tendency for industries to remain in existing locations rather than to move to newer, more attractive locations

**geology** — a science concerned with the study of the earth's crust and the rocks from which it is formed

**glaciers** — slow-moving masses of ice which flow in a stream-like fashion

**gleaning rights** — rights held by common people in Britain, which allowed them to gather leftover grain and wood from the lord's land

**greenhouse effect** — air pollution that acts like a glass shield to trap the sun's heat in the atmosphere, thus causing a gradual rise in the global temperature

**hierarchy** — an organization of persons or things that has higher and lower ranks

**high mass consumption** — a stage in the economic development of a country where incomes are high and the demand for material wealth allows the mass production of consumer goods

**horizontal integration** — a company is horizontally integrated if it controls all parts in the production of a finished product. An automobile company would be horizontally integrated if it manufactured glass, tires, engines, sheet steel, and the other components necessary for producing a car.

**hydrocarbons** — compounds of hydrogen and carbon, especially oil, natural gas, and coal

**import duy** — a tax levied by a government on goods which are imported from other countries

**incentives** — programs giving people or businesses added reasons to buy or provide products or services

**individual freedom** — the freedom to make personal decisions enjoyed by consumers and sellers within a market economy

**individual responsibility** — the responsibilities of consumers and sellers within a market economy to make good economic decisions

**industrial park** — an area set aside by the government in order to attract new industries. These sites often have services such as electricity, water, and sewer lines already established.

**industrial relations** — a term used to describe the working relationship between labour and management in a company

**Industrial Revolution** — a period of social and economic change when societies switched from hand power to machine power for the production of goods. The Industrial Revolution occurred in England in the late 1700s, and then spread to the United States and other countries.

**inflation** — a condition where the cost of living increases as a result of rising prices and wages

**Information Revolution** — a third major revolution in our history (after the Agricultural and Industrial Revolutions) based on the multiplication of new knowledge and use of computers for processing information

**innovation** — a new way of doing things. The market economy has traditionally been viewed as encouraging innovation to ensure products are successful.

**institution** — an established organization that has a specific purpose

**interchangeability of parts** — the production system based on parts made to such a high degree of accuracy and uniformity that they could be interchanged. This was an important step in the development of mass production techniques.

**invisible hand** — an expression used by Adam Smith in his book, *The Wealth of Nations*, in 1776 to explain how the market economy would look after the public good. The theory states that the self-interest of the business community would look after the public interest.

**isohyet** — a type of isoline joining all points on a map which have the same amount of rainfall

**isoline** — a line on a map joining points of equal value. A contour line is one example of an isoline, as it joins all the points which are the same height above sea level.

**isostatic rebound** — the process by which the surface of the land rises after it is relieved of the huge weight of glaciation

**isotherm** — a type of isoline joining all points on a map which have the same temperature

**judicial branch** — the federal courts, including the Supreme Court, which is independent of other government branches and can overturn laws that are deemed to be unconstitutional

**labour** — one of the three factors of production. Labour represents the physical and mental work carried out by employees.

**land** — one of the three factors of production. Land represents the space and physical resources needed to carry out industrial processes.

**landscape region** — an area with common physical and human features

**lapse rate** — the decline in air temperature with increases in altitude

**legislative branch** — the branch of the federal government, consisting of the Congress and Senate, which is responsible for making laws

**liability** — any debt incurred by an individual or corporation

**limited liability** — legal condition that restricts the amount of debt that an individual is required to repay

**lobby group** — a special interest group that tries to influence law makers to make decisions in favour of its cause

**Luddites** — originally a group of workers that organized a number of riots in Britain between 1811 and 1816 for the purpose of destroying machinery. The name is now used to describe any person who wishes to stop progress and turn the clock back.

**manifest destiny** — an expression used by the journalist John O'Sullivan of the *New York Morning News* in 1845. He argued that the United States should expand to eventually occupy all the land in North America.

**manipulate** — to use influence for one's own purpose. Critics of the market economy claim that advertisers manipulate consumers and create artificial demands for products and services.

**market** — a place where buyers and sellers meet

**market economy** — an economic system where decisions are made by individual buyers and sellers

**market gardening** — the growing of fruits and vegetables for sale fresh to consumers

**mass production techniques** — techniques for making large numbers of identical products by machine

**mechanization** — the increasing use of machines to do work normally done by people or animals

**megalopolis** — a large urban area made up of a number of large and small cities that have grown together

**migration patterns** — the patterns created as people move from one country to another and from one region in a country to another

**monopoly** — a market with only one seller. In such situations, the seller can control the market and demand high prices.

**municipal governments** — local government for cities and rural areas

**needs** — basic necessities of life such as food, clothing, and shelter

**nomadic** — the lifestyle of tribes of people that wander the land seeking pasture and water for their flocks

**non-durable goods** — goods consumed directly

**organization** — one of the four characteristics used to describe an institution. Organization refers to the way in which individuals within the institution relate to each other.

**pacifist** — a person opposed to warfare

**particulates** — small particles of solid matter or liquid released into the atmosphere by industrial processes

**partnership** — a business organization owned by two or more people or groups

**patent** — a document from the government granting an individual, often the inventor, the exclusive right to manufacture, sell, or profit from a new product

**permafrost** — permanently frozen ground

**petrochemical industry** — a huge industry which finds and processes petroleum and natural gas to produce products for consumers and industries

**philanthropist** — a wealthy person who helps non-profit groups, such as charities and the arts

**pollution** — the addition of harmful materials to the land, water, or air, which damage the environment

**population growth** — the increase in the number of people living in a country

**power** — one of the four characteristics used to describe an institution. The power of an institution is a measure of its ability to accomplish its goals.

**precipitation** — moisture which condenses out of the atmosphere in the form of rain, hail and snow

**primary industries** — industries based on the extraction of natural resources

**privatization** — the sale of government-owned industries to private owners

**producer** — a person or company who supplies goods or services

**profit** — income from a business enterprise after deducting all costs

**protectionist** — a person who believes that a country should have trade barriers to favour local industries

**public company** — a company whose shares can be owned and freely traded by the general public

**puddling** — the process of stirring molten iron in a furnace so as to turn it into wrought iron

**purpose** — one of the four characteristics used to describe an institution. The purpose of an institution is its primary reason for existing.

**quality of life** — a measure of the economic, social, and aesthetic wellbeing of a country's people

**recycling** — a method of conservation where items such as bottles and newspapers are collected so that the materials can be reused

**reducing agent** — a material which is used to help remove oxygen in an industrial process

**resource** — anything that can be used to create goods or services

**rolling** — a term used to describe a common method of flattening out steel after it has been smelted

**sales** — money generated from the selling of products and services by a business

**San Andreas Fault** — a crack or break in the earth's crust in the Coast Ranges of the United States which marks the boundary between two plates of the earth's surface

**scarcity** — the limited supply of economically important commodities

**secondary industries** — industries that turn semi-finished products (the output of primary industries) into useful consumer goods, such as gasoline, cars, and computers

**secondary sector** — that part of the economy which includes firms which manufacture products

**settlement patterns** — the manner in which people populate the land. Settlement patterns vary from predominantly rural to predominantly urban.

**share** — a unit of ownership in a company that has a certain value

**single proprietorship** — a business owned by one person

**sliding rest lathe** — a machine for cutting high quality screws designed and patented by David Wilkinson

**smelting** — the process of separating iron metal from the rock ore

**smokestack industries** — traditional secondary industries, such as steel mills and factories, that were characterized by the use of coal and petroleum as energy sources

**solid wastes** — a type of pollution produced by municipalities and industries that is neither gaseous nor liquid

**sports** — recreational pastimes and athletic activities which have assumed a major importance within the market economy of the United States

**steam power** — the production of useful power by burning hydrocarbons to create steam pressure. After water power, this was the second source of inanimate power used in the Industrial Revolution.

**strike** — negotiating strategy where workers refuse to work to try to force an employer to reach an agreement

**subsidiary** — a firm owned by a parent company

**supply** — the goods or services sellers are willing to offer for sale to consumers

**supply line** — a line on a chart showing how the supply of a product will change as the price changes

**tariff** — a tax or duty placed on imports

**technology** — scientific knowledge that is applied to create new products and ideas

**telegraph** — a way to send messages through wires using electricity

**temperature** — a measure of the amount of heat in the atmosphere

**tertiary industries** — activities that provide services to consumers, such as sales, nursing, teaching, repairs, and entertainment

**tertiary sector** — that part of the economy which includes firms and industries which provide services rather than manufactured products

**thermal inversion** — when cold air is trapped near the ground by a layer of warm air above it

**traditional economy** — an economic system where decisions are made on the basis of tradition

**tree line** — a line beyond which trees do not grow because of the lower temperatures at high altitudes and latitudes

**trigger industry** — an industry which catapults a country into economic development and eventually produces self-sustaining growth

**tundra** — a grassy, treeless plain occurring in the most northerly parts of the North American continent and at high altitudes

**vegetation** — plant life

**venture capital** — money invested by individuals and governments in new, high-risk businesses. Those providing such money usually expect a higher return on their capital because of the risk involved.

**vertical integration** — a company is said to be vertically integrated if it controls all aspects of production from the processing of raw materials to the assembly of the final product

**wants** — those things people desire but do not need for survival

**water frame** — a machine invented by Sir Richard Arkwright and powered by water that was used for spinning cotton

**wrought iron** — a malleable form of iron which has had the non-metallic impurities removed and has then been rolled or forged

# Index

Acid rain, 117
Advertising, 103-109
Affirmative action, 126
Agriculture, 2-6
Air pollution, 115-118
Aircraft, commercial, 59
Algae, 118, 119
Alluvial soil, 43
Altitude, 48
American Heart Association, 94
American War of Independence, 18
Amtrak, 59
Annexations, 53-54
Annual meeting, 72
Annual report, 72
Anoxic water, 118
Antitrust legislation, 33, 107
Appalachian Mountains, 42
Apple Computer Company, 95-96
Arctic Coastal Plain, 46
Assembly line, 34
Assets, 73
Atari, 96
Athletes, 129-131
Attorney-general, 71
Automation, 78
Automobile industry, 31, 34-36, 61
Automobile transportation, 58-59

Banks, 13, 74-75
Boom and bust, 30
Business, role of, 71-74
Buyers, 83, 85-86

Canadian Shield, 46
Canals, 12
Capital, 8, 84-85, 96
Carson, Kit, 29
Cast iron, 13
Catalytic cracking, 31
Change, predictions of, 137-140
Chavez, Cesar, 78
Civil rights, 127

Civil Rights Act, 125
Clean Water Act, 120
Climatic influences, 47-50
Coastal Lowlands, 45-46
Collateral, 96
Collective bargaining, 77
Commercial banks, 74-75
Commission, 99
Common land, 4
Computers, 95-97
Conglomerate, 73
Congress, 68
Constitution, the, 68, 124, 125
Construction industry, 61
Consumers, 35-36, 82-83, 87,
    102-108
Continental divide, 44
Contracts, 71
Corporations, 71-74
Cosmetics, 98-100
Cottage industry, 6
Cotton gin, 20
Credit unions, 74
Crop rotation, 5

Declaration of Independence, 113
Defence spending, 131-133
Demand line, 86
Department of Commerce, 141
Department of Justice, 71
Direct sales, 98
Discrimination, 125-128
Division of labour, 3
Drilling, 30
Durable goods, 61
Duty, 8, 73

Earthquakes, 46
Economic development, 56
Economic power, 18
Economics, 83
Economy, market, 82-89, 106
Efficiency, 87

Electric light bulb, 31
Electricity, 31
Embargo, trade, 18
Employment, 61
Enclosure Acts, 3-5
Engine, gasoline, 34
    steam, 26
Entitlement programs, 131
Entrepreneurs, 8, 85, 90-100
Environment, 114-123, 137-138
Environmental Protection Agency
    (EPA), 120, 122
Equal Credit Opportunity Act, 125
Equal Employment Opportunity
    Commission, 127
Equal Rights Amendment (ERA), 126
Equality of opportunity, 124-127
Equilibrium price, 86
Expansion, 53-60
Exports, 141

Factors of production, 85
Factory system, 7-9
Fads, 105-106
Farms, 3-5
Fast foods, 91-94
Federal Aid Highway Act, 59
Federal budget, 67
Federal government. See
    Government, federal
Federal Reserve System, 70
Flying shuttle, 6
Ford, Henry, 34-36
Ford Foundation, 36
Foreign investment, 73
Foreign subsidiaries, 73
14th Amendment, 125
Franchises, 72, 93, 130
Free market economy, 32, 88
Free trade, 141
Freedom, 87, 124
Frost Belt, 59
Fuel, 62

Gasoline, 31
Gasoline engine, 34
Geography, economic, 53-65
  *human*, 52-64
  *physical*, 40-57
Geology, 40
Ginning, 20
Glaciation, 43-44, 46
Gleaning rights, 4
Goods, 61, 83
Government, branches of, 68-70
Government, federal
  *budget process*, 133
  *Civil Rights Act*, 125
  *Congress*, 68
  *Department of Justice*, 71
  *Equal Credit Opportunity Act*, 125
  *Equal Rights Amendment (ERA)*, 126
  *executive branch*, 68
  *House of Representatives*, 69
  *interference*, 120
  *judicial branch*, 68
  *legislative branch*, 69
  *pollution control*, 122
  *Senate*, 69
Government, municipal, 70
Government, role of, 67-71
Government, state, 70
Government institutions, 68-70
Government regulations, 67,
  106-107, 116
Great Plains, 43
Greenhouse effect, 118
Gulf-Atlantic Coastal Lowlands
  and Piedmont, 42
Gun control, 133-134

High mass consumption, 35
"High-tech" industries, 60
Highways, 59
Homestead Act, 56
Horizontal integration, 32
Hunting, 2
Hydrocarbons, 44

IBM, 96
Import duties, 73

Incentives, 27
Incineration, 114-115
Indians. *See* Native peoples
Individual freedom, 87
Individual responsibility, 87
Industrial parks, 62
Industrial relations, 36
Industrial Revolution, 6-23
Industrialists, 24-36
Industries
  *automobile*, 34-36, 61
  *changes in*, 6-14
  *construction*, 61
  *development of*, 18-37
  *"high-tech"*, 60
  *location*, 61, 63
  *oil*, 29-33
  *primary*, 40, 60
  *railroad*, 25-29
  *secondary*, 60
  *service*, 64
  *"smokestack"*, 60
  *tertiary*, 61
  *textile*, 6
  *transportation*, 11-12
Inflation, 70
Information Revolution, 14
Inland transportation, 22
Innovation, 87
Institutions, 67
Interchangeability of parts,
  21
Interior and Great Plains, 43
Interior Highlands, 43-44
Intermontane Basins and
  Plateaus, 44-45
Interstate Highway System,
  59
Intervention, government,
  116, 122-123
Investment, foreign, 73
"Invisible hand", 113
Iron making, 13, 60
Isoline, 49
Isostatic rebound, 46
Isoyets, 49
Isotherms, 51

Kay, Mary, 91, 98-99
Kerosene, 29, 31
King, Martin Luther Jr., 127

Labour, 84
  *cost of*, 61
  *division of*, 3, 21
  *role of*, 76-78
Labour force, 76-78
Labour organizations, 76-79
Land, 84
  *acquisition of*, 53-54
  *common*, 4
Land grants, 58
Land pollution, 114
Land treaties, 54
Landfill, 114
Landscape regions, 41-47
Lapse rate, 48
Lead pollution, 116
Lending banks, 13
Lewis, John L., 77
Life, quality of, 8, 113-114
Limited liability, 71
Loans, 13
Lobby groups, 122, 133
Louisiana Purchase, 53
Luddites, 8

Machine tool industry, 18
Managers, 100
Manifest destiny, 55
Manufacturing industries, 61-62
Market economy. *See*
  Economy, market
Market gardening, 46
Markets, 18, 61, 83, 139
Mary Kay Cosmetics, 98-99
Mass production, 18-21, 34
Materials, raw, 61
McDonald's Restaurants, 91-94
Mechanization, 76
Meeting, annual, 72
Migration patterns, 59
Military spending, 131-134
Mills, 8
Mineral deposits, 43

Minorities, 125-128
Mixed market economy, 88
Money, supply of, 70
Monopolies, 33, 107
Municipal governments. *See*
  Governments, municipal
Muskets, manufacture of, 21

Nader, Ralph, 106
National Women's Party, 126
Native peoples, 56
Natural resources, 42-47
Needs, 83
Nomads, 3
Non-durable goods, 61

Ocean, 48-49
Oil industry, 25, 29-33
Oil wells, 30
Opportunity, equality of, 124-127
Organizations, labour, 76

Pacific Railroad Act, 27, 58
Pacific Ranges, 45
Pacifism, 36
Packaging, 122
Parks, industrial, 62
Particulates, 115
Partnerships, 71
Passenger transportation, 58-59
Patents, 6, 26
Permafrost, 46
Pesticides, 120
Petrochemical industry, 31
Philanthropy, 36
"Pink-collar ghetto", 126
Pipelines, 31
Planting, methods of, 5
Plastics, 121
Pollution
  *air*, 115-118
  *land*, 114-115
  *lead*, 116
  *prevention*, 121-123
  *water*, 118-120
Pony Express, 57
Population, distribution of, 59

Post-Colonial period, 18
Power, 11, 62
Poverty, 127-128
Precipitation, 49
Price, equilibrium, 86
Primary industries, 40, 60
Privatization, 137
Producers, 83, 109
Production, factors of, 85
Profit, 75
Profit-sharing, 36
Proprietorships, single, 71
Protectionism, 141
Public Citizen Health
  Research Group, 94
Public company, 13
Puddling process, 13
Purchasing power, 105

Quality of life, 8, 113-114, 124-126

Railroad, transcontinental, 44, 58
Railroad industry, 25-29
Railroad transportation, 25-29
Railroads, 57-59
Raw materials, 18, 61
Recycling, 121-122
Reducing agents, 63
Refining, 31
Regulations, government,
  67, 107-108
Regulations, safety, 107
Reservations, 57
Resource, 84
  *natural*, 42-47, 60
Responsibilities,
  consumer, 107
Responsibility,
  individual, 87
Restaurants
  *drive-in*, 91-93
  *fast-food*, 92-94
Retail stores, 74
Revolution, Industrial.
  *See* Industrial
  Revolution
Rights, consumer, 107

Road transportation, 11-12
Roadbuilding, 11
Robots, 78, 139
Rock formations, 43
Rockefeller, John D., 32-33
Rocky Mountains, 44
Rolling process, 13

Safety standards, 106-107
Sales, 73, 98
San Andreas Fault, 46
Savings banks, 74-75
Scarcity, 83
Sears, Roebuck and
  Company, 74
Secondary industries, 60
Security, national, 124
Seeding, 5
Sellers, 83, 85, 87
Senate, 69
Service industries, 64
Service sector, 138
Services, 83
Settlement patterns, 55-57
Shares, 13, 71
Sherman Antitrust Act, 33
Single proprietorships, 71
Sliding rest lathe, 19
Small arms industry, 18
Smelting, 13
Smith, Adam, 113
"Smokestack"
  industries, 78
Social welfare, 8
Solid wastes, 114, 121
Sovereignty, consumer, 103
Spinning jenny, 6
Sports, 129-131
Stagecoach service, 57
State government. *See*
  Government, state
Statehood, 54
Steam engines, 22, 26
Steam locomotives, 26
Steam power, 11
Steamboat, 19
Steamboat navigation, 22

Steel manufacture, 60, 141
Stocks, 71
Submarine, 22
Subsidiaries, 33, 73
Sun Belt, 59, 138-139
Supply and demand, 29, 32
Supply line, 86
Supreme Court, 68

Tariffs, 141
Teamsters, 31
Technology, 76, 90, 141
Telegraph, 57
Temperature, 47-49
Tenant farms, 5
Tertiary industries, 61
Textile industry 6-9, 18, 25
Thermal cracking, 31
Tourism, 60
Trade barriers, 141

Trade embargo, 18
Traditional economy, 85
Trains. *See* Railroads
Transcontinental
    railroad, 27, 44
Transportation, 11-12, 21-22,
    25-29, 57-59
    *air*, 59
    *automobile*, 58-59
    *railroad*, 57-59
Treaty of Guadalupe-Hidalgo, 54
Tree line, 44
Trigger industry, 25
Trust, Standard Oil, 32
Tundra, 46

Unions, 77-79

Values, 113-114, 124-134
Varignon frame, 63

Vegetation, 50
Venture capital, 96
Vertical integration, 32, 34
Volcanic Islands of
    Hawaii, 46

Wages, 61, 76, 78
Wants, 83
Wastes, solid, 114, 121
Water frame, 7
Water pollution, 118-120
Water power, 18
Water transportation,
    18, 21-22
Water-craft, 22
Welfare, 57
Whitney, Eli, 20-21
Women workers, 125-127
Work force, 76-78
Wrought iron, 13

# Sources

**Figure 3.4** *Historical Atlas of the United States*, Centennial Edition (Washington, D.C.: National Geographic Society, 1988), pp. 196-200.

**Figure 4.1** Stephen S. Birdsall and John W. Florin, *Regional Landscapes of the United States and Canada*, 3rd ed. (New York: John Wiley & Sons, Inc., 1985), p. 22.

**Figure 4.2** Lewis Paul Todd and Merle Curti, *Triumph of the American Nation* (Orlando: Harcourt Brace Jovanovich, 1986), pp. 1020-1021.

**Figure 4.3** Lewis Paul Todd and Merle Curti, *Triumph of the American Nation* (Orlando: Harcourt Brace Jovanovich, 1986), pp. 1020-1021.

**Figure 4.6** Robin E. Crickmer and William Hildebrand, *The United States* (Toronto: Holt, Rinehart & Winston of Canada, Limited, 1972), p. 49.

**Figure 4.7** Robin E. Crickmer and William Hildebrand, *The United States* (Toronto: Holt, Rinehart & Winston of Canada, Limited, 1972), p. 49.

**Figure 4.8** Robin E. Crickmer and William Hildebrand, *The United States* (Toronto: Holt, Rinehart & Winston of Canada, Limited, 1972), p. 51.

**Figure 4.9** Joseph R. Conlin, *A History of the United States: Our Land, Our Time* (San Diego: Coronado Publishers, 1985), p. 819.

**Figure 5.1** Joseph R. Conlin, *A History of the United States: Our Land, Our Time* (San Diego: Coronado Publishers, 1985), p. 818.

**Figure 5.2** Lewis Paul Todd and Merle Curti, *Triumph of the American Nation* (Orlando: Harcourt Brace Jovanovich, 1986), p. 1002.

**Figure 5.7** Nigel Barber, *A New Nation: The American Experience* (Toronto: McGraw-Hill Ryerson, Limited, 1989) p. 170.

**Figure 5.8** Joseph R. Conlin, *A History of the United States: Our Land, Our Time* (San Diego: Coronado Publishers, 1985), p. 818.

**Table 5.1** Otto Johnson, executive ed., *Information Please Almanac Atlas & Yearbook 1989*, 42nd ed. (Boston: Houghton Mifflin Company, 1989).

**Figure 5.11** Joseph R. Conlin, *A History of the United States: Our Land, Our Time* (San Diego: Coronado Publishers, 1985), pp. 824-825.

**Table 6.1** Otto Johnson, executive ed., *Information Please Almanac Atlas & Yearbook 1989*, 42nd ed. (Boston: Houghton Mifflin Company, 1989), p. 56.

**Table 6.2** Otto Johnson, executive ed., *Information Please Almanac Atlas & Yearbook 1989*, 42nd ed. (Boston: Houghton Mifflin Company, 1989), p. 56

**Table 6.3** Otto Johnson, executive ed., *Information Please Almanac Atlas & Yearbook 1989*, 42nd ed. (Boston: Houghton Mifflin Company, 1989), p. 57.

**Table 6.4** Otto Johnson, executive ed., *Information Please Almanac Atlas & Yearbook 1989*, 42nd ed. (Boston: Houghton Mifflin Company, 1989).

**Table 6.5** Otto Johnson, executive ed., *Information Please Almanac Atlas & Yearbook 1989*, 42nd ed. (Boston: Houghton Mifflin Company, 1989), p. 59.

**Table 6.6** Otto Johnson, executive ed., *Information Please Almanac Atlas & Yearbook 1989*, 42nd ed. (Boston: Houghton Mifflin Company, 1989), p. 64.

**Figure 6.10** *World Book Encyclopaedia* (Chicago: World Book Inc., a Scott Fetzer Company, 1986), Vol. 12, p. 11.

**Table 6.7** *World Book Encyclopaedia* (Chicago: World Book Inc., a Scott Fetzer Company, 1986), Vol. 12, p. 11.

**Table 8.2** *RCALL Food Selection Guide*, Virginia Polytechnic Institute and State University, Publication 642. Revised 1975; Catherine F. Adams, *Nutritive Value of American Foods in Common Units*, Agriculture Handbook No. 456, 1975; Barbara Kraus, *The Dictionary of Sodium, Fats, and Cholesterol.*

**Figure 10.3** Dr. Thomas F. Bowman, Dr. George A. Giulani, and Dr. M. Ronald Minge, *Finding Your Best Place to Live in America* (New York: Red Lion Books, 1981), p. 269.

**Figure 10.7** *Time*, August 1, 1988, pp. 42-43.

**Figure 10.9** *World Book Encyclopaedia* (Chicago: World Book Inc., a Scott Fetzer Company, 1986), Vol. 6, p. 260.

**Table 11.1** Otto Johnson, executive ed., *Information Please Almanac Atlas & Yearbook 1989*, 42nd ed. (Boston: Houghton Mifflin Company, 1989).

**Table 11.2** Otto Johnson, executive ed., *Information Please Almanac Atlas & Yearbook 1989*, 42nd ed. (Boston: Houghton Mifflin Company, 1989).

**Figure 11.2** *Calgary Herald*, February 7, 1989, p. A4.

**Figure 11.5** *Calgary Herald*, December 3, 1988, p. C3.

**Table 11.4** *Calgary Herald*, 1988.

**Table 11.5** U.S. Department of Labor, December 1987.

**Figure 11.7** Pamela Chibucos, *Economic Choices: Political Decisions that Affect You* (Arlington, Va: The Close Up Foundation, 1987), p. 48.

**Figure 11.8** Stockholm International Peace Research Institute, 1988.

**Figure 12.1** U.S. Department of Commerce.

**Figure 12.2** *Calgary Herald*, April 16, 1989, p. A6.

**Figure 12.4** U.S. Department of Labor.

**Figure 12.5** Pamela Chibucos, *Economic Choices: Political Decisions that Affect You* (Arlington, Va: The Close Up Foundation, 1987), p. 64; Commercial Atlas and Marketing Guide (Rand McNally and Co., 1989).

**Figure 12.6** *International Labour Review*, Vol. 125, No. 1, January/February 1986, p. 43.